New Accents

General Editor: TERENCE HAWKES

READING TELEVISION

* Not available from Methuen, Inc. in the USA

JOHN FISKE and
JOHN HARTLEY

READING TELEVISION

METHUEN
LONDON AND NEW YORK

First published in 1978 by Methuen & Co. Ltd
11 New Fetter Lane, London EC4P 4EE
Reprinted 1980 and 1982

Published in the USA by
Methuen & Co.
in association with Methuen, Inc.
733 Third Avenue, New York, NY 10017

Printed in Great Britain by
Richard Clay (The Chaucer Press) Ltd,
Bungay, Suffolk

ISBN 0 416 85560 1

To Natasha and Clare

CONTENTS

GENERAL EDITOR'S PREFACE

I T is easy to see that we are living in a time of rapid and radical social change. It is much less easy to grasp the fact that such change will inevitably affect the nature of those academic disciplines that both reflect our society and help to shape it.

Yet this is nowhere more apparent than in the central field of what may, in general terms, be called literary studies. Here, among large numbers of students at all levels of education, the erosion of the assumptions and presuppositions that support the literary disciplines in their conventional form has proved fundamental. Modes and categories inherited from the past no longer seem to fit the reality experienced by a new generation.

New Accents is intended as a positive response to the initiative offered by such a situation. Each volume in the series will seek to encourage rather than resist the process of change, to stretch rather than reinforce the boundaries that currently define literature and its academic study.

Some important areas of interest immediately present themselves. In various parts of the world, new methods of analysis have been developed whose conclusions reveal the limitations of the Anglo-American outlook we inherit. New concepts of literary forms and modes have been proposed;

new notions of the nature of literature itself, and of how it communicates are current; new views of literature's role in relation to society flourish. *New Accents* will aim to expound and comment upon the most notable of these.

In the broad field of the study of human communication, more and more emphasis has been placed upon the nature and function of the new electronic media. *New Accents* will try to identify and discuss the challenge these offer to our traditional modes of critical response.

The same interest in communication suggests that the series should also concern itself with those wider anthropological and sociological areas of investigation which have begun to involve scrutiny of the nature of art itself and of its relation to our whole way of life. And this will ultimately require attention to be focused on some of those activities which in our society have hitherto been excluded from the prestigious realms of Culture.

Finally, as its title suggests, one aspect of *New Accents* will be firmly located in contemporary approaches to language, and a continuing concern of the series will be to examine the extent to which relevant branches of linguistic studies can illuminate specific literary areas. The volumes with this particular interest will nevertheless presume no prior technical knowledge on the part of their readers, and will aim to rehearse the linguistics appropriate to the matter in hand, rather than to embark on general theoretical matters.

Each volume in the series will attempt an objective exposition of significant developments in its field up to the present as well as an account of its author's own views of the matter. Each will culminate in an informative bibliography as a guide to further study. And while each will be primarily concerned with matters relevant to its own specific interests, we can hope that a kind of conversation will be heard to develop between them: one whose accents may perhaps suggest the distinctive discourse of the future.

TERENCE HAWKES

ACKNOWLEDGEMENTS

ANY book that attempts to break new ground is liable, unless it can rely upon unusually strong and resilient support, to get stuck in the mud. To our general editor, Terence Hawkes, without whose constant help this book would no doubt have suffered just such a fate, much thanks.

We are also grateful to Stuart Hall, Director of the Centre for Contemporary Cultural Studies at the University of Birmingham, for his formative comments on an earlier version of our work on *News at Ten*. David Bevan of the Polytechnic of Wales has read, heard and modified our arguments throughout their formulation with more patience than some of them deserved, and Sheila Griffiths was instructive in the section on dance. We must also thank our colleagues Sue Power and Pat Gerrish, who typed the manuscript. To them and the rest of our colleagues at the Polytechnic we owe a better book. We would wish to incriminate none of them, however, in any mud that still clings.

We owe more than can be written in books to our respective partners, Natasha and Clare.

Finally we must thank our students at the Polytechnic of Wales for their cheerful if sometimes forthright reactions to our thesis, and their toleration of our questions and question-naires.

J.F., J.H.

1 'READING' TELEVISION

Argu. for

IN August 1976, the British Broadcasting Corporation produced a programme to celebrate forty years of television entitled *What do you think of it so far . . . ?* The answer to that catchphrase question (known to every fan of TV comedians Morecambe and Wise) is 'Rubbish!' Evidently the BBC is as dubious as some of its critics about the quality of its output over the years. In the face of such modesty from the oldest broadcasting institution in the world, it would perhaps be rash to assert the contrary judgement – that television's customary output may be just as good in its own terms as Elizabethan drama and the nineteenth-century novel were in theirs.

However, if we are to go by some of the criticisms made about Elizabethan theatres and dramatists by their own contemporaries, we can see that those closest to the scene do not always make the best judgements. After all, Shakespeare himself was called 'an upstart crow' who 'supposes he is as well able to bombast out a blank verse as the best of you' by a fellow playwright, Robert Grene. And some of the most respectable citizens in the country considered that the Shakespearean theatres left something to be desired:

> They are the ordinary places for vagrant persons, Maisterles men, thieves, horse stealers, whoremongers, Coozeners,

Coneycatchers, contrivers of treason and other idele and daungerous persons to meet together . . . They maintaine idlenes in such persons as haue no vocation & draw apprentices and other seruants from their ordinary workes and all sortes of people from the resort vnto sermons and other Christian exercises to the great hinderance of traides & pphantion of religion. (Cited in Harbage 1941, pp. 84–5)

Television has been accused of many (though by no means all) of these crimes by its own contemporary critics. And yet, like the Elizabethan theatres, it is a familiar and popular experience for a large proportion of people from all sections of society.

Since the seventeenth century, Elizabethan drama has been subjected to a great deal of scrutiny, and early judgements such as the ones we have mentioned are now considered perhaps a little hasty. What is lacking in respect of television is this same kind of scrutiny. Television productions may be as good as those of the Elizabethan theatre, but we have no fully formed language of appreciation to 'read' them by. The tools of literary and dramatic appreciation are by now very sophisticated. But these tools will not necessarily do for television. Just as literature is not the same 'thing' as drama (and so you cannot 'read' a Shakespeare play in the same way as you would read a nineteenth-century novel), so television as a medium differs from both. Furthermore, television is a characteristic product of modern industrial society, while literature and the theatre come down to us from societies whose structures and organization were different. True, both have had to adapt to the modern world – but one of the features of that world is television.

Hence the tools of traditional literary criticism do not quite fit the television discourse. At best they can be used in the way a metaphor works – the unknown tenor of television might be apprehended by means of the known vehicle of literary criticism. But even here there are problems, one of the most fundamental of which is the difficulty in recognizing that literature and television are two different types of media. Every medium has its own unique set of characteristics, but the codes which structure the 'language' of television are much more like those of speech than of writing. Any attempt to decode a television 'text' as if it were a literary text is thus not only doomed to failure but is also likely to result in a negative evaluation of the medium based on its inability to do a job for which it is in fact fundamentally unsuited.

But we live in a society where literacy and its associated skills and modes of thought are valued very highly. This means that the tendency to judge all media, including television, by the prescriptions of literacy is not the result of mere intellectual confusion. Rather it is a reflection of dominant cultural values, instilled during five hundred years of print-literacy. Furthermore, it is a tendency that is not confined to television's critics. The consequent habits of thought have encouraged those people who control and encode the television message (people who are drawn largely from the most literate sections of society) to attempt to preserve literate values within the medium.

This is an example of what McLuhan calls 'rearview-mirrorism' – where a new medium explores its potential in terms of the medium it is in the process of supplanting. Television is to some extent subversive of the very values most prized by literacy, which perhaps explains the uneasiness felt by the BBC about its achievements over forty years of broadcasting. The written word (and particularly the printed word) works through and so promotes consistency, narrative development from cause to effect, universality and abstraction, clarity, and a single tone of voice. Television, on the other hand, is ephemeral, episodic, specific, concrete and dramatic in mode. Its meanings are arrived at by contrasts and by the juxtaposition of seemingly contradictory signs and its 'logic' is oral and visual. We shall attempt to show how the contradiction between literate and non-literate modes of thought derives from social and historical conditions and how it has helped to shape the form of television discourse. In other words, before we can arrive at a language of appreciation appropriate to television, we must formulate an idiom which takes account of the singularity of the medium, and of its place in history.

In the chapters that follow, we aim to show how much of this work is already under way. It may look at first as though we are taking a sledge-hammer to a rather insignificant nut – after all, everybody *knows* what it is like to watch television. Certainly; and it is television's familiarity, its centrality to our culture, that makes it so important, so fascinating, and so difficult to analyse. It is rather like the language we speak: taken for granted, but both complex and vital to an understanding of the way human beings have created their world. Indeed, the resemblance of television discourse to spoken language explains our interest in the communicative role played by television in society.

We shall try to show how the television message, as an extension of our spoken language, is itself subject to many of the rules that have been shown to apply to language. We shall introduce some of the terms, originally developed in linguistics and semiotics, that can help us to identify and successfully decode the sequence of encoded signs that constitutes any television programme. The medium itself is both familiar and entertaining, but this should not blind us to its singularity. As Diamond (1975) has rightly pointed out:

> Television's detractors argue that it is the 'boob tube', that it requires a minimum of intelligence to use ('You don't even have to know how to read'). Actually, television is a very demanding mode of communication. Television's information is ephemeral; there is no way for the viewer to go back over material, in the way a newspaper reader or book reader can glance back over the page. (p. 64)

In other words, we should not mistake an oral medium for an

illiterate one. We have the example of Shakespeare to remind us that non-literate entertainment can be as demanding, and satisfying, as the most profound works of literature.

In later chapters we shall consider the place of television in society. The way it communicates with its audience can be likened to what happens if, when flicking through the pages of this book, you were to come across letters in print resembling your own name. All the other words escape your attention as your eye scans the fast-moving information, but your name is deeply imprinted on you: you are primed to recognize its familiar form even when you are unaware that you have been 'reading' the information. In the same way the television medium presents us with a continuous stream of images *almost all* of which are deeply familiar in structure and form. It uses codes which are closely related to those by which we perceive reality itself. It appears to be the natural way of seeing the world. It shows us not our names but our collective selves.

It does this so 'naturally' that discussion of the process might seem to be superfluous. But it is at that point that discussion in fact becomes most crucial. Television is a human construct, and the job that it does is the result of human choice, cultural decisions and social pressures. The medium responds to the conditions within which it exists. It is by no means natural for television to represent reality in the way that it does, just as it is by no means natural for language to do so. Both language and television *mediate* reality: there is no pristine experience which social man can apprehend without the culturally determined structures, rituals and concepts supplied to him via his language. Language is the means by which men enter into society to *produce* reality (one part of which is the fact of their living together in linguistic society). Television extends this ability, and an understanding of the way in which television structures and presents its picture of reality can go a long way towards helping us to understand the way in which our society works.

Hence the television discourse presents us daily with a constantly up-dated version of social relations and cultural perceptions. Its own messages respond to changes in these relations and perceptions, so that its audience is made aware of the multiple and contradictory choices available from day to day which have the potential to be selected for future ways of seeing. Of course, the picture does not appear to be so fluid as we watch: there are 'preferred' meanings inherent in every message. But even preferred meanings, which usually coincide with the perceptions of the dominant sections of society, must compete with and be seen in the context of other possible ways of seeing. These 'active contradictions' in the television message serve to remind us of our culture's daily state of play. (Good examples of this process can be found in a *News at Ten* bulletin, analysed in detail in chapters 6 and 8.)

This social function can no longer be performed by other art forms such as the novel, especially on the mass scale available to television. It is often claimed that certain great artists, for instance Joyce, Kafka, Brecht, or Sterne in *Tristram Shandy*, are able to 'defamiliarize' the established conventions of thought and perception. Defamiliarization is a term borrowed from Russian Formalist criticism (see Lemon and Reis 1965). It describes the way these writers hesitate or hold back from producing sense in their messages, thereby demonstrating the arbitrary nature of the codes with which we are familiar. They thus demystify our perception of reality, which emerges as 'real-seeming', rather than as reality itself. The effect of this effort, it is claimed, is to confront the reader with his true place in the ideological framework of his society. Defamiliarization rescues the individual from a 'consumerist' role. The inclusion of such 'messages' as *Ulysses* or *The Trial* or *The Resistible Rise of Arturo Ui* into the stream of products of the novel or theatre genres serves to isolate the conventions of the mainstream and thus expose them to view.

Television is widely held to be unsuited to this kind of

role. It is taken to be wholly commercial, conventional and conservative. But this is only another way of saying that as a medium it is normative, a casual part of everyday experience. In fact, it is the very familiarity of television which enables it, according to our analysis, to act as an agency for defamiliarization. It is, indeed, more suited to this role than many of the great critical works of literature because contradictory perceptions are structured into all its messages, and we are not encouraged by any shaping artistic vision to learn to live with them. Furthermore artists like Brecht and Joyce are to some extent frustrated in their intentions by the fate of their products, which have been, as it were, re-mystified by the constant admiration which is their unhappy lot. It is difficult for a reader to use a great work of art for purposes of shattering, reforming and reproducing the established norms when the work in question has been incorporated into these norms.

Television is certainly aware of the arbitrariness of many of its own codes, and while not criticizing them, certainly celebrates them. What we, the audience then *do* with the message is another matter. We are certainly not suggesting that we are constantly and consciously defamiliarizing the message *in order* to criticize or isolate the ideological framework within which we live. What we do suggest is that taking television as we find it, we, the audience, are spontaneously and continuously confronted with this framework and must negotiate a stance towards it in order to decode and thus enjoy the entertainment in which it is embodied.

Hence the kind of analysis which has read Joyce and Kafka without 'reading' television eventually denies to the ordinary viewer the power – even the possibility – of recognizing for himself his own situation in all its complexities and contradictions. The television message, on the other hand, is forced by its own constraints and internal contradictions to accord just this freedom of perception to all its viewers. In other words, we do not need to impose changes on the television message in order to produce defamiliarization; rather we should, as critics, learn to understand what it is that the language of television is saying to us.

2 CONTENT ANALYSIS

What's there

THE starting-point of any study of television must be with what is actually there on the screen. This is what content analysis is concerned to establish. It is based upon the non-selective monitoring, usually by a team of researchers, of the total television output for a specified period. It is not concerned with questions of quality, of response or of interpretation, but confines itself to the large scale, objective survey of manifest content. However, the reading of television must progress from the *manifest* content to the *latent* content, and very few analysts have begun to tread this path.

None the less, it is clearly important to establish what is, in fact, there, even though the individual viewer will watch only a fraction of it. It is also worth pointing out that a global view can correct the inevitable imbalance of the individual's experience of the medium. One of the earliest major studies of television content was made by Smythe in 1953. Smythe analysed all the drama programmes broadcast in New York City in the first week of January of that year. He found, among other things, that drama concentrated on people in their courting or child-bearing ages and portrayed disproportionately few of the young or old. The characters worked in professional, middle-class jobs rather than in routine white-collar or blue-collar ones, and males outnumbered females by 2:1. This sexual discrimination was repeated in the heroes of stories, where males again outnumbered females by 2:1, but among villains the male dominance was 4:1. Villains tended to be older than heroes, and were less likely to be white Americans. Only ten blacks were portrayed during the week, eight of whom were in minor roles, while the other two were heroes.

De Fleur (1964) studied six months' output of drama on television in a midwestern town in the early 1960s. He was interested in how the world of work was represented on television, how it compared with the real world of work in America, and the sort of attitudes it might form in children about their future careers. His findings supported many of Smythe's: for instance that ordinary jobs of modest prestige were held by half of the actual labour force, but by only 10 per cent of the TV labour force, and that there was a corresponding over-representation of high-prestige jobs. This was especially true for males, well over half of whom on television held jobs of high prestige.

This sort of descriptive study can provide useful data about the content of television output as a complete 'message system'. The researchers are cautious about inferring much of socio-cultural significance from them, but Smythe wonders if the fact that villains are older than heroes might represent, to a society that values youth with its physical activity and sexuality, the menace of an older generation that holds on to its social power despite physical decline. A currently popular series, *Starsky and Hutch*, suggests a similar contemporary pattern.

But despite their caution, most researchers do make some references from the message system of television to the society that produces it and to which the message responds. Where they differ is in the way they see the relationship between the two. De Fleur argues that:

Television presents *least often* and as *least desirable* (from a child's standpoint) those occupations in which its younger viewers are most likely to find themselves later ... Television may be instructing children in ways that are not readily apparent even to close observers – ways that may lead to later disappointments as the individual enters the labour force. (1964, pp. 69–70)

This implies that the world of work on television *should* represent the real world of work precisely, and that because it does not, it distorts reality. It also implies that children in particular and viewers in general react to the message system in the same way as they react to the reality that it portrays.

Gerbner disagrees with both these implications when he argues that 'to be "true to life" in fiction would falsify the deeper truth of cultural and social values served by symbolic functions' (1973b, p. 268); or again, 'The symbolic world is often very different from the "real" world ... The power and significance of symbolic functions rests in the *differences*' (1973a, p. 571). In the same vein, Hall (1973) recognizes that messages about violence and violence itself are different in kind, and he argues that violence in the television western is ultimately about social relationships and behaviour; it signifies professional, skilled, cool conduct, resolving a crisis.

So, when De Fleur (1964) tells us that one third of the jobs represented on television were involved with the enforcement or administration of the law, we might better see this as a reflection of social values, not of objective social reality. Other sections of De Fleur's study give us hints of what one meaning of this apparent over-representation may be. In a survey of children's attitudes towards work he found that what a large majority of them most valued in an occupation was its capacity to exert power over others. This was followed by money, prestige, travel and the opportunity to help others, in that order. He then constructed an 'index of power' by which he could give each job on television a 'power value', which reflected the proportion of dominant acts to submissive ones. This showed that all those concerned with the law had power values well above average, with judges, attorneys and police officials being the most powerful of all television occupations; their power values were exceeded only by the more rarely represented occupations of foremen, ranch owners and clergymen.

So we might infer that television's over-representation of particular occupations may not be a distortion of reality, but may reflect the esteem given in our social value system to power over others, particularly when it is exerted by white males in their physical prime. We must note here that some of the most popular law-enforcement heroes of the 1960s and early 1970s, while being white and male, were deliberately shown *not* to be in their physical prime (see below, p. 175).

The world of television is clearly different from our real social world, but just as clearly related to it in some way. We might clarify this relationship by saying that television does not represent the manifest actuality of our society, but rather reflects, symbolically, the structure of values and relationships beneath the surface. So the high proportion of middle-class occupations is not a distortion of social fact, but an accurate symbolic representation of the esteem with which a society like ours regards such positions and the people who hold them.

Blacks and women

The world of work has received much attention from television content analysts because of the importance our society places on a man's occupation in establishing his social place. Seggar and Wheeler (1973) found that an analysis in terms of sex and race of occupational roles portrayed on television in 1971 produced some interesting results. Some things had not changed since the earlier studies – the over-portrayal of men and of middle-class occupations – but the portrayal of non-whites had increased significantly.

This would seem to reflect a change in the cultural value system, for non-whites were not only represented more often, but also in jobs of higher prestige. Among major male characters, there was no difference in prestige between blacks and whites, but among females, black women were on average of higher prestige than whites (see table 1 below for details).

This relatively favourable treatment of racial minorities was prefigured in an earlier study by Head (1954), which showed that although racial minorities were portrayed lower down the social scale than whites, they were slightly less likely to be criminal and significantly less likely to be presented unfavourably: only 4 per cent of blacks were bad, and only 8 per cent portrayed unsympathetically.

The fact that racial minorities are treated more favourably in the symbolic world of television than in society may indicate that the liberal desire to integrate them socially is ahead of the social fact, and that television is playing an active role in this ongoing social change. If this is so, then the outlook for women is less optimistic, at least in the early 1970s, for the content analysis of television shows sexual differentiation to be at least as important as that of race or class.

Seggar and Wheeler (1973) studied job stereotyping and found that blacks and women were shown in fewer occupations than whites and men: 57 per cent of black males and 65 per cent of black females worked in the five most frequently portrayed occupations whereas the figures for whites were 29 per cent and 50 per cent respectively. As an interesting point of comparison we may note that the stereotyping of British females on American television was even narrower, with 70 per cent in the five most common occupations (41 per cent as nurses, 12 per cent as secretaries, and the other 17 per cent divided equally among maids, actresses and government diplomats). Seggar and Wheeler compared five races (white Americans, blacks, chicanos, British and Europeans) and both sexes. They found significant racial differences, but even larger sexual ones. Women are, in the symbolic world of television, more socially disadvantaged than members of racial minorities.

The actual occupations are interesting; the five most frequently portrayed for white and black American males and females were:

Table 1

White male (N = 1112)	%	Black male (N = 95)	%	White female (N = 260)	%	Black female (N = 20)	%
physician	7·6	government	18·9	secretary	15·5	nurse	30·0
policeman	7·6	diplomat		nurse	15·0	stage/dancer	15·0
musician	4·8	musician	13·7	stage/dancer	8·1	musician	5·0
serviceman	4·6	policeman	9·5	maid	6·5	government	5·0
government	4·5	guard	9·5	model	5·0	diplomat	
diplomat		serviceman	5·3			lawyer	5·0
						secretary	5·0
	29·1		56·9		50·1		65·0

N = total numbers in each category. (Seggar and Wheeler, 1973, p. 212)

The most striking difference between the races in the males is the reversal between government diplomat and physician, but there is no real difference of status of occupation. In the female lists, however, the higher status occupations of government diplomat and lawyer appear only for black females, and the lower ones of maid and model only in the whites. But, clearly, the major status differentiation is between the male and female lists.

Unfortunately we cannot use De Fleur's power index to compare these jobs accurately in terms of their power over others, for he uses different job categories. But if we match them as far as possible, we find that all the male occupations have a positive power index value, with the exception of 'enlisted military personnel' – a subcategory of 'servicemen'; and all the female occupations have a negative value with the exception of 'lawyer', and lawyers rate below police and physicians. So white females rarely, if ever, appeared in occupations that allowed them to exert power over others, though 10 per cent of black women and most of the black men did.

Dominick and Rauch (1972) studied the image of women in television advertisements screened in 1971 and found, not surprisingly, that the same social value system was evident. Women were portrayed in fewer occupations than men, and those occupations had negative power index values. The top three occupations for males and females in the world of advertisements in 1971 were:

Table 2

Females (N = 230)	%	Males (N = 155)	%
housewife/mother	56	husband/father	14
stewardess	8	professional athlete	12
model	7	celebrity	8
	71		34

(Adapted from Dominick and Rauch, 1972, p. 263)

What is significant here is that there is a considerable difference between the actual occupations in drama and advertisements, but no difference in the structural relationship of male to female in terms of job stereotyping and power. The advertisement analysis supported earlier drama analyses by finding a high proportion of people (71 per cent) in the 20 to 35-year-old category.

Since these analyses in the early 1970s there have been at least three major series – *Police Woman, Bionic Woman* and *Charlie's Angels* – which give women the law-enforcement or investigative roles normally reserved for men. Angie Dickinson, the star of *Police Woman*, has explicitly related this to the changing role of women in society. This change of job-role, however, does not necessarily disturb the established way in which our society views women. We shall elaborate this point in our discussion of *Bionic Woman* in chapter 12.

Drama and social values

Head, in his 1954 analysis of series drama on television, found that the typical setting was in a contemporary (82 per cent), American (88 per cent) city (76 per cent), with by far the commonest category being crime–detection–adventure (37 per cent), followed by situation comedies (22 per cent). Of the characters who were classifiable by class, 85 per cent were upper and middle class, though 26 per cent of protagonists and 20 per cent of antagonists were unclassifiable. This social centrality of values is underlined by the congruence of the ethical and affective status of characters, for good characters were presented sympathetically 90 per cent of the time, and non-sympathetically only 4 per cent of the time. Bad characters were presented sympathetically only 6 per cent of the time, but non-sympathetically 90 per cent of the time.

Head also considers the role of the major characters as protagonists and antagonists. Every play, by definition, has a protagonist, but 41 per cent have 'non-personalized antagonists' (NPAs); that is, antagonists who are an aspect of the protagonist's own self, or of his situation, or of fate. Character weaknesses are the commonest NPAs (63 per cent), fate is next with 27 per cent and only 10 per cent come from the social situation. Interestingly, NPAs never occur in children's drama, and in only 9 per cent of crime-detection plays, but they perform a central function in 82 per cent of situation comedies.

When an antagonist is personalized he is likely to be significantly older than the protagonist, and very likely to be a professional criminal. Criminals are potent social symbols, for 72 per cent of those shown are major characters in the drama series, whereas only 56 per cent of non-criminal characters are major. We shall return to this later but for the moment it is worth noticing Head's suggestion that the criminal in police series and the NPA in situation comedies have structural similarities, in that they both enact the negative values of our social value system. Interestingly, Gerbner's (1970) study, which we discuss in more detail below, suggests that the main difference between heroes and villains is the greater efficiency of the heroes and the sympathy with which they are presented. Otherwise, there are few clear-cut distinctions, particularly in morality or method. What the police versus criminal conflict may enact symbolically, then, is the everyday conflict of a competitive society in which efficiency is crucial. The loser is therefore to some degree socially deviant and thus appropriately represented, in terms of the social value structure, as a criminal. The common concern that television police are becoming more and more like the criminals in their methods and morals, means that the few factors that do distinguish them take on crucial significance. Of these distinctive features, efficiency is the most marked.

Violence and our culture

The view that the content of the television message system is a representation of the underlying values of society is articulated most fully by Gerbner in a number of publications. A good example of this is his report (1970) of the study he made with his colleagues at the Annenburg School of Communications, of violence in television drama. Head had opened the question of the role of violence in his 1954 study when he found that the commonest act of violence in television drama was battery, closely followed by homicide, pointing a deadly weapon, aggravated assault and fraud. In real life, murder is one of the least common crimes, and is considerably rarer than rape – which did not occur at all in the dramas studied by Head. The form of violence presented with most approval was the pointing and firing of guns, the least approved involved drugs and sex offences, theft and homicide. It would appear that television violence is not the same as real violence. This is supported by Larsen *et al.* (1963) in their analysis of goals and methods of achieving them in television drama. Of their eight categories of such methods, violence is by far the most common (32·6 per cent of the methods portrayed). This is followed by 'organizational' methods, involving negotiation, co-operation and compromise (only 12·0 per cent). 'Legal' methods, involving the processes of law, comes third with 9·7 per cent. So we must look for a symbolic rather than a direct relationship between televised fiction and reality. This is precisely what Gerbner does.

In 'Cultural indicators: the case of violence in television' (1970), Gerbner is concerned with the mass-produced messages of television as an active part of our cultural and social environment. He argues that fully to understand the television message we need to study four dimensions of it:

1 *Existence:* What *is* television output (or that of any mass medium), how much of what content and how frequently is it made available to us, are the sort of questions that this dimension of the study aims to answer.
2 *Priorities:* What is important, how prominent, intense or central are certain factors or elements?
3 *Values:* What value judgements are implied about which elements in the cultural message system?
4 *Relationships:* What is related to what, what are the structural meanings of the message?

On the whole, early content analysts tended to concentrate on the first and second dimensions, though, as we have seen, it is often the questions in the third, and especially the fourth that lead us to the more revealing latent meaning. Head approaches the question of ethical value judgements, but it is only Gerbner and his colleagues who have systematically tried to study all four, and in so doing to relate the symbolic world of television to the social world of reality in a way that takes note of their difference in kind.

First, then, Gerbner established the *existence* of violence on television. He found, for example, that 80 per cent of drama contained violence, that 50 per cent of leading characters committed violence and 60 per cent were victims of it. The average week contained 400 casualties, most of whom were killed, stunned or maimed without much visible hurt. Incidentally, studies of British television output show that it contains only 50 to 60 per cent of the violence of American television.

Gerbner found, too, that older people were more likely to be the victims, and younger ones the perpetrators. For instance, one young adult gets killed for every five killers in his age group, whereas there is one middle-aged corpse for every two middle-aged killers. For the old, there are two killed for every killer. The same sort of age discrimination appears in the number of killers who are themselves victims of violence. One young adult killer out of fourteen is himself killed, for middle-aged killers the ratio is 1:5, and for old killers it is 1:1.

In class and race there are again favoured and disadvantaged groups. As we might expect, it is best to be middle-class white, for this is the group least likely to commit or suffer violence. In fact 50 per cent of upper- and middle-class characters committed violence, but 75 per cent of the lower classes did; 60 per cent of the upper- and middle-class suffered violence, 90 per cent of the lower class did. There were three middle-class killers for every middle-class corpse, but for both the upper and lower classes, the ratio was 1:1. About 30 per cent of middle-class characters escaped violence (either as agents or victims) entirely; none of the lower-class characters did.

In terms of race, the figures showed that 50 per cent of white Americans committed violence, compared to 60 per cent of white foreigners, and 67 per cent of non-whites. Victims of violence were of the same order, ranging from 60 per cent of whites to 80 per cent of non-whites. Only 39 per cent of white Americans were both perpetrators of violence and victims, compared to 46 per cent of white foreigners and 60 per cent of non-whites. The same pattern was repeated for those who were neither 'violent' nor victims (35, 32 and

13 per cent respectively). However, when Gerbner looked at the proportion of killers, he found a significant change in the pattern, for one out of five white foreigners were killers, one out of eight white Americans were, and only one out of fifteen non-whites. He noted an 'efficiency factor' at work here distinguishing the superior performance of white violents from that of non-whites. Another dimension of this 'violence efficiency' appeared in the study of the ratio of killers to corpses, which ranged from 4:1 for white Americans, through 3:2 for white foreigners, to 1:1 for non-whites.

In another study, Gerbner (1972) related the violence/victimization ratio to race and sex. In all categories, victimization was more common than violence; but the category with the highest victimization ratio (that is the proportion of victims to aggressors) was that of non-white females, closely followed by non-white animal characters in cartoons, whereas the safest category was that of white males, with animal cartoon characters of no apparent race coming second. The most aggressive, in terms of the acts of violence committed, were animal characters of no apparent race, followed closely by non-white males. The least aggressive were white and non-white females. Gerbner comments: 'Crude as they are, these patterns begin to lay bare some assumptions cultivated in these message systems' (1970, p. 75).

The extent of violence in the content of drama has already established its high ranking in Gerbner's second dimension, the *priorities* of televised drama. Hardly a play, and hardly a character is free from it.

On the third dimension, that of *values*, Gerbner has less to say. The values by which society judges violence often in fact emerge most clearly from a study of the fourth dimension, or the way that violence is structured into the drama. However, Gerbner considers that cross-cultural studies may in future provide a fruitful way into the study of the values of the mass message system. As an example he cites an international film study that he made in 1969, which revealed that the ratio of the tendency to commit socially sanctioned violence to anti-social violence was 2·5 : 1 in France, 2·6 : 1 in the USA, 3·5 : 1 in Italy, 3·8 : 1 in Czechoslovakia, 4·1 : 1 in Yugoslavia and 4·4 : 1 in Poland (the lower the ratio, the higher the proportion of violence rated as anti-social).

But it is on the fourth dimension of *relationship and structure* that some of his most significant findings occur. Most violence was impersonal, strangers assaulting each other for power, private gain or duty. It was interpersonal, at close range, but rarely involved intimates. The good initiated violence as often as the bad, but they hurt less and killed less, and suffered more violence themselves. The bad, of course, are the ultimate losers, but on the way to their deserved ends they were hurt less. Half of all those who killed, in fact, were heroes who reached a happy end in their dramas.

Gerbner then used personality differential scales to identify the key differences between violents and nonviolents, between those who had a happy fate and those who did not (or, for most practical purposes, between heroes and villains) and between killers and killed. Non-violents were rated as more normal and more attractive than violents, but less logical, less efficient and more emotional. This also made them appear less masculine. In the distinction between violents and killers, the killers appeared markedly more efficient and slightly less emotional, thus supporting Gerbner's idea of a 'violence efficiency factor'.

People with a happy fate, broadly the heroes, are distinguished from the unhappy-fated, or villains and victims, mainly by being rated virtuous and attractive whether violent or not. The unhappy-fated are repulsive when violent and emotional when not.

In the killers/killed differentiation, the key differences occur on the attractiveness and efficiency scales. Heroes (killers with a happy fate) are markedly more attractive and efficient than victims or villains (killers with an unhappy fate).

In general, all violents are more logical than non-violents; the key to violence with a happy fate is efficiency; unhappy-fated killers and victims are presented as bunglers. Violents are also the most masculine, and the victims the least masculine and the oldest.

The attractiveness of the hero correlates with his happy fate and his efficiency; 'violence does not mar, nor non-violence improve, the attractiveness of the hero', comments Gerbner, who goes on to sum up the implications of his findings thus: 'Cool efficiency, and, to a lesser extent, manliness and youth, appear to be the chief correlates of success and virtue in a fairly impersonal, self-seeking and specialized structure of violent action' (1970, p. 78). He concludes that violence is not a matter of simple behaviour, and that television portrayals of it mirror rather than illuminate our society's prejudices. The television message system is, he suggests, a system of 'cultural indicators' by which the value-structure of society is symbolically represented.

Violence, then, is used in the pursuit of the socially validated ends of power, money or duty, and is *inter*personal although *im*personal: that is, takes place between strangers. So despite its obvious connection with power or dominance over others, it is not the dominance of one personality over another, but of one social role over another social role. It is linked to socio-centrality, in that the victims are likely to belong to less esteemed groups, defined in terms of age, class, sex and race, and the successful aggressors are likely to be young, white, male and middle-class or unclassifiable. Violence is not in itself seen as good or evil, but when correlated with efficiency it is esteemed, for efficiency is a key socio-central value in a competitive society. Violence on television, then, is not a direct representation of real-life violence. Unlike real violence, its internal rules and constraints govern what it 'means' in any particular context to the observer, rather than to the combatants themselves. Its significance in a television fiction is that it externalizes people's motives and status, makes visible their unstated relationships, and personalizes impersonal social conflicts between, for example, dominant and subordinate groups, law and anarchy, youth and age. It is never a mere imitation of real behaviour.

In other words, all the evidence of content analysis points us to a crucial distinction between violence in televised drama and real violence, and it should make us aware of the inaccuracy of the commonly held belief that these are similar in performance and effect. Television violence is encoded and structured into a governed relationship with the other elements of the drama; this relationship is controlled by rules which are themselves derived from social values, and which are common to all television texts in their particular genre. Our familiarity with the genre makes us react to violence according to its own internal rules, and not as we would to real violence. We know, as we approve of the death of the socially deviant villain under a hail of socio-central police bullets, that we would not approve in the same way if the equivalent real-life villain were gunned down in front of us. The difference in our reaction is not explained by saying that a death on television is weaker, less perceptually imperative, for the difference is one of kind, not of degree.

It is at this level that violence is seen as a complex system of signs of behaviour, more or less efficient, by which the socio-central hero and deviant villain enact the competitive relationship of their roles. The policeman/detective hero is a sign of socio-centrality; the criminal/victim becomes, then, the social deviant, not only because criminal behaviour is by definition deviant, nor because criminal/victim status correlates with deviant groups – the wrong sex, class, race or age – but also because, in a competitive society, inefficiency or bungling is deviant. The criminal is distinguished from the hero primarily by his inefficiency and his social group; his morals, methods and aims are the same.

Content analysis can tell us much about television, but not everything. Gerbner sums up well when he writes:

I must stress again that the characteristics of a message system are not necessarily the characteristics of the individual units composing the system. The purpose of the study of a system *as system* is to reveal features, processes and relationships expressed in the whole, not in its parts. Unlike most literary or dramatic criticism (or, in fact, most personal cultural participation and judgement), this approach to message-system analysis focuses on the record of institutional behaviour in the cultural field, and on the dynamics of message-production and image-cultivation in a community but not necessarily in selective personal experience and response. (1969, p. 128)

So content analysis does not help us to respond to the individual programme, nor, more importantly, the viewing session; it does not help us with matters of interpretation nor with how we respond to the complex significance and subtleties of the television text. That sort of reading of television requires that we move beyond the strictly objective and quantitative methods of content analysis and into the newer and less well explored discipline of semiotics.

3 THE SIGNS OF TELEVISION

SEMIOTICS, simply defined, is the science of signs; how they work and the ways in which we use them. Semiology is another word for the same science, and currently each is used by different authorities with much the same meaning. We shall use semiotics, though semiology will appear in some of our quotations. The lack of agreement on terms by its main practitioners is symptomatic of the youth of semiotics as a discipline, and of its lack of a common origin. The need for such a science was predicted both by the Swiss linguist Saussure (1974), with whose work the term semiology is associated, and by the American philosopher Pierce (1931–58), who coined the term semiotics. Subsequent writers have developed their work with an increasing proliferation of terms; a much tangled growth which one can begin to unravel by referring to a companion volume in the New Accents series, Hawkes's *Structuralism and Semiotics* (1977).

However, although the terms may vary, the central concerns of semiotics may be stated simply. They are two: the relationship between a sign and its meaning; and the way signs are combined into codes. In this chapter we shall be concerned with signs, in the next with codes: in both we shall attempt to relate the theory of semiotics to the practical world of television.

The sign, the signifier and the signified

Ferdinand de Saussure, who is commonly regarded as the European father of semiotics, was the first to elaborate the tripartite concept *signifier + signified = sign*. The *signifier* is a physical object, e.g. a sound, printed word or image. The *signified* is a mental concept (bearing no *necessary* relationship to the signifier). The *sign* is the associative total which relates the two together. We must stress that this sort of analytical breakdown is for convenience only. There can be no signifier distinct from a signified and neither of these can exist outside the construct we call a sign. All three elements of this composite construct, then, are determined by our culture, or are, in some sense, man-made.

Iconic, motivated signs

In the iconic or motivated sign there is a natural relation between the signifier and signified. Thus a portrait or a photograph is *iconic*, in that the signifier represents the appearance of the signified. The faithfulness or accuracy of the representation, that is the degree to which the signified is re-presented in the signifier, is an inverse measure of how conventionalized it is. Thus a realistic portrait is lightly conventionalized: it relies for its ability to signify on our experience of the sort of reality that it re-presents. A photograph of a street scene communicates easily because of our familiarity with that sort of reality: if the photograph is taken from the top of a high building, we have to go through a more conscious interpretative process, referring to our memory of bird's-eye views. If, to take the illustration further, the photograph is one taken from a reconnaissance aircraft, it requires specialist decoding by men who have learnt the codes within which such signs operate. The more closely the signifier reproduces our common experience, our culturally determined intersubjectivity (see below, p. 46), the more realistic it appears to be. But we must be at pains to emphasize that the signified to which the signifier relates is itself arbitrary, for the way we see it, categorize it and structure it is a result of our culture's way of seeing, just as much as the way we reproduce it in verbal language. The signified is determined by our culture, not by some external natural reality.

Given this important gloss on the nature of the signified, it is still useful to recognize that in the iconic sign it exerts a strong influence or constraint upon the form of the signifier, and this constraint is called *motivation*. In general, the greater the motivation, the smaller the role played by socially based convention; and the weaker the motivation, the more constraining is the convention.

The form of the signifier, then, can be determined either by the signified or by convention. In highly motivated signs, the signified is the determining influence, in signs of low motivation, convention determines the form of the signifier. Thus the form that a photograph of a car can take is determined by the appearance of the specific car itself; on the other hand, the form of the signifier of a generalized car on a traffic sign is determined by the convention that is accepted by the users of the code. So the weaker the motivation, the more determining the convention has to be, until we reach a point where the motivation has disappeared and the sign has become *unmotivated* or *arbitrary*.

Arbitrary, unmotivated signs

In this type of sign the signifier relates to its signified by convention alone, by an agreement among its users that this sign shall mean this. Words are, of course, our commonest arbitrary signs: there is no necessary relation between a word and its meaning. Hence we may not understand a Frenchman's arbitrary verbal sign for CAR, but we can understand his motivated road signs in so far as they are iconic. The primacy of the iconic sign on television can tempt us to ignore the arbitrary nature of much of the medium's signification. There are a few clearly arbitrary signs, such as a 'dissolve' which signifies a remembered scene is to follow, or a slow-motion shot which signifies either analytical appreciation when used in sports programmes or lyrical beauty when used in drama or advertisements. But the arbitrary or conventional dimension is often disguised by the apparent natural iconic motivation or realism of the sign: hence a shot from ground level of a tall building *conventionally* signifies that the next scene will take place in an office or flat in that building; a man in a detective drama showing the inside of his wallet is *conventionally* a sign of a policeman identifying himself and not, for instance, of a pedlar of dirty postcards. In this last example, the sign clearly started life as iconic and motivated: policemen really do do this, but by frequent repetition its motivated dimension has decreased and its arbitrary, conventional dimension has increased.

Even the most iconic signs must have an arbitrary dimension: or, to put it another way, the apparently motivated quality of the television sign must not blind us to the equally central role of convention in conveying its meaning.

The three orders of signification

This sort of discussion of signs can only go so far towards explaining how they convey meaning, for it has concentrated on the sign as a self-contained construct. A photograph or a road sign can both be signs of a car, but the photograph, semiotically, can go further; it can also be a sign of virility or of freedom, and in certain contexts it can even be used to signify an industrial, materialist and rootless society. We are clearly involved with a far more complex idea of 'meaning' than the simple relationship between the photograph and the car itself. There are different levels of meaning or, to use the semiotic term, different *orders of signification*.

The first order of signification is the one we have discussed so far. In this order the sign is self-contained, the photograph *means* the individual car. In the second order of signification this simple motivated meaning meets a whole range of cultural meanings that derive not from the sign itself, but from the way the society uses and values both the signifier and the signified. In our society a car (or a sign for a car) frequently signifies virility or freedom. The range of cultural meanings that are generated in this second order cohere in the third order of signification into a comprehensive, cultural picture of the world, a coherent and organized view of the reality with which we are faced. It is in this third order that a car can form part of the imagery of an industrial, materialist and rootless society.

Barthes, in *Mythologies* (1973) and *Elements of Semiology* (1968), discusses in some detail the way signs work in these different orders of signification. To follow his ideas we must introduce some more technical terms. According to Barthes, signs in the second order of signification operate in two distinct ways: (1) as *myth-makers* and (2) as *connotative agents*. We shall study both in some detail because they are crucial to an understanding of the way television conveys its full meaning.

Second-order signs I : myths

To explain Barthes's theory of 'myth' we can turn to a news-film from the ITN programme *News at Ten*, of 7 January 1976. (We will be making extensive reference to this bulletin throughout the rest of the book.) Illustrating an item of news about troop reinforcements in Northern Ireland, it shows British soldiers in Belfast patrolling the streets, defending their sandbagged positions, and operating with a helicopter and armoured troop carriers. This film will enable us to explain the second order of signification and how it derives from the first.

When a sign carries cultural meanings rather than merely representational ones, it has moved into the second order of signification. In this movement the sign changes its role; the *sign* of the particular soldier becomes the *signifier* of the cultural values that he embodies in this news-film. The 'cultural meaning' of the soldier is what Barthes calls a *myth*.

Thus, the image in our film of a soldier clipping a magazine on to his rifle as he peers from his sandbagged bunker fortress in Belfast can activate the myth by which we currently 'understand' the army. This myth, as we shall show, is that the army consists of ordinary men, doing a professional and highly technological job. In order to trigger this myth the sign must be robbed of its specific signified, in this case, perhaps, of 'Private J. Smith, 14.00 hours, January 4, 1976'. The sign loses this specificity and becomes now the second-order signifier; so the signified becomes 'one-of-our-lads – professional – well-equipped' (not Private J. Smith), and the sign in this second order activates or triggers our mental 'myth chain' by which we apprehend the reality of the British soldier/army in Northern Ireland.

The myth is validated from two directions: first from the specificity and iconic accuracy of the first-order sign, and second from the extent to which the second-order sign meets our cultural needs. These needs require the myth to relate accurately to reality out-there, and also to bring that reality into line with appropriate cultural values.

The myth of the British army that is in fact being appealed to is what we may call the currently established one – the army as 'our lads, as professional, and as technologically well-equipped'. The ITN news reporter-cameraman chooses three main signs to activate this myth chain by which the army is apprehended. First, the camera dwells in close-up on individual soldiers peering out of the fort or dug-out at an undefined, unillustrated enemy. We look over the soldiers' shoulders, we share their position, and thus their role as one-of-us, defending us and ours, is immediately identified. Basically the same sign occurs frequently in popular war films or in the traditional western, where 'white hat' defends the fort/homestead/wagon train against 'black hat' or Indians. News reporting and fiction use similar signs because they naturally refer to the same myths in our culture.

The next aspect of the myth is that of the soldiers as the professionals – well-trained, special people. This is the myth the army itself propagates in its recruiting campaigns. One sign activating this myth is a shot of soldiers issuing from the heavy double gates of the fort into a suburban street. They move in a ritualistic, crouching glide, in a predetermined order to predetermined positions. Here, again, the image of the soldier as a specially trained person, identified by special behaviour, can be seen operating in other aspects of our culture such as films or children's play.

This second aspect of the myth is closely linked to the third, which is that of the army's technological expertise and glamour – again, a familiar image. The camera dwells on a helicopter rising over an urban skyline for no other reason than that it is an army helicopter. The camera shows us more of the visual thesaurus of war – automatic rifles, troop-carriers, armoured Land Rovers.

These three visual signs then cohere into an overall myth of the army as our lads, professional and well-equipped. But this coherence is perhaps better expressed as a *conceptual movement*, for the myths of the army are not apprehended in their totality in a single moment of awareness, but rather in a chain of concepts along which our responses move. The sign which starts our responses along this chain is acting like a *metonym* (see below); it is a part which stands for the whole.

The other characteristic of myths that we must stress is their dynamism. They are constantly changing and up-dating themselves, and television plays an important role in this process. It constantly tests the myths against reality and thus shows when their explanatory power has decreased and the need for change becomes more pressing.

Our news-film from Belfast provides us with a particularly clear example of the way television can hint at the inadequacy of our present myths and thus contribute to their development. The sequence of army shots is followed immediately by a sequence showing the funerals of some of the victims of the violence. The last shot of the army sequence is of an armoured troop-carrier moving right to left across the screen. There is then a cut to a coffin of a victim being carried right to left at much the same pace and in the same position on the screen. The visual similarity of the two signifiers brings their meanings into close association. The coffin contains the death that should have been prevented by the soldiers in the troop-carrier. Thus the myth of the army that underlies the whole army sequence has been negated by television's characteristic of quick-cutting from one vivid scene to another. We may well see this as a small contribution to changing the myth of the British army by bringing to it the concept of gallant failure, if not defeat.

Second-order signs II: connotation

We have already noted that there are two second-order sign systems: myth is one and *connotation* the other. Let us begin to explain this connotative order of signs with a simple example. A general's uniform *denotes* his rank (first-order sign), but *connotes* the respect we accord to it (second-order sign). We could, for instance, conceive of a uniform that became steadily more ragged and poverty-stricken as the rank of the holder increased: a general's ragged uniform would still denote his rank, but the connotative meaning would have changed radically. In the connotative order, signs signify values, emotions and attitudes.

Barthes, in an essay entitled 'The Rhetoric of the Image' (1977), argues that in photography the denoted meaning is conveyed solely through the mechanical process of reproduction (denotation is visual transfer), while connotation is the result of human intervention in the process – camera distance/angle, focus, lighting effects, etc. Connotation is expressive, involving subjective rather than objective experience, and is essentially the way in which the encoder transmits his feelings or judgement about the subject of the message. Metz (1974) takes a similar view:

> In American gangster movies, where, for example, the slick pavement of the waterfront distils an impression of anxiety and hardness . . . the scene represented (dimly lit, deserted wharves, with stacks of crates and overhead cranes) . . . and the technique of the shooting, which is dependent on the effects of lighting in order to produce a certain *picture* of the docks . . . converge to form the signifier of connotation. The same scene filmed in a different light would produce a different impression; and so would the same technique used on a different subject (for example, a child's smiling face). (p. 97)

Television uses much the same methods as film to connote meaning: camera angle, lighting and background music, frequency of cutting are examples. Music in particular is used to clarify and sometimes create the connotative meaning of a shot. A sign of a man about to open a door can connote suspense and anxiety by the addition of conventional suspense music, or a shot of an empty room can be made to connote either eeriness or peace by the music and lighting. Berger, in *Ways of Seeing* (1972), has shown how the connotative meaning of a televised painting can be changed by the background music accompanying it. The connotative dimensions of signs in a conventional medium like television tend to be more limited and explicit, some would say crude, than in the more aesthetic media like the art film or even poetry. But they are still an important part of the way television signifies. We discuss the role of connotation more fully in our analysis of an extract from *Cathy Come Home* with which we end this chapter.

The third order of signification

In considering both second orders of signification we have moved away from a view of the sign as an independent entity, and have entered the realm of subjective responses. Though these responses occur in the individual, they are not, paradoxically, individualistic in nature. Since they are invoked by signs which mean what they do only through agreement between the members of the culture, they are centred in that ill-defined area we call *intersubjectivity*. This is the area of 'subjective' responses which are shared, to a degree, by all members of a culture. We can no more decide that the lighting and style of representation of Metz's waterfront connotes joy and freedom rather than anxiety and hardness, than we can decide that the word *banana* refers to a four-legged animal, or that the myth of the British army activated by the signs of the soldiers in Northern Ireland is the myth of triumphant conquerors freeing the world from a tyrant. This intersubjectivity is culturally determined, and is one of the ways in which cultural influences affect the individuals in any culture, and through which cultural membership is expressed.

The myths which operate as organizing structures within this area of cultural intersubjectivity cannot themselves be discrete and unorganized, for that would negate their prime function (which is to organize meaning): they are themselves organized into a coherence that we might call a *mythology* or an ideology. This, the third order of signification, reflects the broad principles by which a culture organizes and interprets the reality with which it has to cope.

Elsewhere (Hartley and Fiske 1977) we have shown how the mythology which organizes the *News at Ten* bulletin from which our Belfast news-film is taken has to do with the relationship between major social institutions and the individuals within them. A number of institutions are presented during the course of the programme: the British army (in Belfast); the navy (in the 'Cod War' with Iceland); the government (throughout, but especially as financier of the housing programme and as employer of National Health Service doctors); major employers (in this case the British Steel Corporation); and foreign governments (American,

Spanish and Italian). All of them are shown to be responding to crises bravely enough. But their efforts ultimately
seem inadequate and are presented as being doomed to
failure. However, the individuals working within these
institutions are shown to be acting as positively and as effectively as their institutional contexts will allow. Hence dis-
illusionment with major institutions *as such*, coupled with an
undiminished respect for the individual, would appear on
the evidence of this typical bulletin to be a crucial part of
our contemporary mythology.

Metaphor and metonymy

Barthes's theories concentrate on how signs relate to the
culture that uses them, and while this is obviously a crucial
relationship, we must balance it by a more detailed look at
how signs convey meaning and the ways in which they
relate to each other.

Metaphor and *metonymy* are terms that will be relatively
familiar to students of literature. Traditionally, a metaphor
is a word (signifier) which is applied to an object or action
(signified) to which it is not literally or conventionally
applicable. For instance, New Yorkers often call their city
'The Big Apple'. The connection between 'New York' and
'apple' is not natural, it is *asserted*. Of course, asserted metaphors may themselves become conventional, as in the
expression 'New York *appeals* to me'. A metonym is the
application of a mere attribute of an object to the whole
object. For instance many Londoners call their city 'The
Smoke'. Smoke used to be a characteristic part of the London scene, resulting in the smogs which were called (meta-
phorically) 'pea-soupers'. It came to signify the city as a
whole, but this time the relationship between the signifier
(Smoke) and its signified (London) is *contiguous* rather than
asserted.

The way we use the terms metaphor and metonymy in
this book derives from (though it is not quite the same as)

Jakobson's theories of poetics rather than from traditional literary criticism.[1] Jakobson (1958) and Leach (1976), among others, broaden the scope of the two terms. They see metaphor and metonymy as the two fundamental modes by means of which the meanings of signs are conveyed. According to this broad view, metaphor involves a transposition or displacement from signified to signifier, together with the recognition that such a transposition implies an equivalence between these two elements of the sign. Clearly, then, *all* signifiers are by that token metaphorical, to the extent that at the first order of signification they involve a constructed equivalence between the sign and the reality it represents. Hence we can extend the notion of metaphor to non-verbal signifiers, and think in terms of 'visual metaphors'. These are constructed, as opposed to asserted. Thus, a portrait of a man is constructed in such a way as to convince us that the two-dimensional visual representation is equivalent to its three-dimensional reality. Similarly a map, or a scale model, signifies the reality to which it refers by constructing an equivalent form in whose features we can recognize those of the object itself. Thus both verbal and non-verbal, arbitrary and iconic signs can be metaphorical. When we come to discuss television realism in chapter 11, it will be important to remember that an apparently direct or iconic representation of reality is more accurately a metaphorical reconstruction of that reality in the terms of the television medium. The similarity we perceive between signifier and signified should be thought of as a *constructed equivalence*; the metaphoric real world shown on television does not *display* the actual real world, but *displaces* it.

In metonymy, on the other hand, the signification depends upon the ability of a sign to act as a part which can signify the whole. For instance Victorian entrepreneurs got

---

[1] We have in fact conflated into our usage of the term metonymy another very similar function described by the rhetorical term *synecdoche*. This is the figure of speech in which part is named but whole is understood, or vice versa.

into the habit of referring to their wage-labourers as 'hands';
taking a significant attribute of the people involved to
signify those people. You can see that metonymy, like metaphor, is capable of modifying its user's perception of the
signified. If an employer reduces people to their hands,
being the attribute he values in them, it is perhaps more
difficult for him even to perceive other attributes which they
may have.

Metonymy is also capable of making physical objects
signify quite abstract concepts. For instance, a crown is an
object, part of the regalia associated with monarchs. The
'crowned heads of Europe' are often said to be gathered
together on great occasions: we can safely assume they are
accompanied by the remaining items of their bearers'
anatomies. However, the crown is also a metonymic sign for
sovereignty. Its signified includes not only the rest of the
royal regalia but also extends to the more abstract notions
of the monarchy, imperialism and a particular form of social
order.

Television signs can operate simultaneously in both the
metaphoric and the metonymic mode, but each mode performs a different function. In the first order of signification,
the iconic or denotative function of the sign is metaphoric.
It involves the transposition from reality to representation,
so that on the level of manifest content (i.e. the denotative
order), a shot of a city street is a constructed metaphor of the
specific street itself. But it is also and predominantly a
metonym of the whole city or of 'city-ness', for the realism
of much television drama results from the metonomy of its
setting at the level of manifest content.

However, in the second order of signification, in latent
content, it is the metaphoric mode which tends to dominate.
We can now see that the over-portrayal of white-collar jobs
on television is simply a metaphor of their place in our
culture's hierarchy of esteem. Here the transposition is from
one plane, that of social values, to another, that of frequency
of representation. The equivalence is constructed (though

disguised and not foregrounded for inspection as is the case in asserted metaphor), and is connotative, not denotative.

Television advertisers are particularly adept at exploiting both metaphoric and metonymic modes in order to cram as much meaning as possible into a thirty-second slot. The sign of a mother pouring out a particular breakfast cereal for her children is a metonym of all her maternal activities of cooking, cleaning and clothing, but a metaphor for the love and security she provides. In this case, the transposition or deplacement is from an affective plane to a material one. (In the case of the over-portrayal of white-collar jobs the transposition is from the plane of representing values to that of representing facts.) The metonym, on the other hand, involves contiguity – giving breakfast is actually part of the set of maternal activities.

The structural relationship between these two modes can be visualized as operating on two axes, one 'vertical' and the other 'horizontal' in character;

selective/associative (or paradigmatic) dimension
(metaphor)

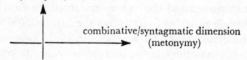

combinative/syntagmatic dimension
(metonymy)

Paradigms and syntagms

You will observe that we have introduced two new terms into the above diagram: *paradigmatic* and *syntagmatic*. Briefly, a paradigm is a 'vertical' *set* of units (each unit being a sign or word), from which the required one is selected. A syntagm is the 'horizontal' *chain* into which it is linked with others, according to agreed rules and conventions, to make a meaningful whole.

Paradigms and syntagms are fundamental to the way that any system of signs is organized. In written language, for instance, the letters of the alphabet are the basic vertical paradigms. These may be combined into syntagms called words. This example illustrates other properties of the terms. The units in a paradigm are distinct and separate from each other (the letter 'a' is not like the letter 'b'), but when combined into a syntagm they can be modified according to their relationship with other units. Thus a letter can have its sound changed by the letter following it (witness the 'o' in the words 'shop' and 'show'), or it can even change its form in some languages (Welsh mutations are a good example). On the next level of organization, we can see that the words of a language form a paradigm which we call its vocabulary. These words can then be formed into syntagms called phrases or sentences according to the rules of grammar.

These are formal paradigms and syntagms, but the same dimensions of analysis can be seen in less formally defined situations. There are, for instance, paradigms of words appropriate to a 'legal document', a 'family meal time' or even a 'night out with the boys'. These paradigms, which in linguistics are called *registers*, are established by convention and usage, and are thus relatively more flexible than the paradigm of the words of the language itself (which changes very slowly).

A paradigm itself is defined by a certain similarity between its units – for example, words appropriate to 'a family meal time'. But within the paradigm, the units are clearly distinguished from each other. Thus, a unit in a paradigm has two dimensions of meaning: its relationship with and at the same time distinctiveness from its fellow units. The second dimension is the more crucial; a unit's meaning is defined in opposition to others in its paradigm, and we therefore understand a sign by contrasting it with what it is *not*.

Thus, to understand fully the signs of the myth of the British army which we discussed earlier, we must contrast them with signs and myths that they are not. Some examples of the paradigm we must refer to, that of other 'signs and myths of an army', are juxtaposed in *Scoop, Scandal and Strife*, a collection of news photographs edited by Baynes (1971). They include the British soldier in World War I, sitting outside a French cottage with a bouncing baby on his knee; the dead machine gunner lying twisted beneath a belt of bullets, his shirt open to reveal a white chest with a streak of blood across it; the citizen of Prague baring his chest before the muzzle of the gun of an advancing Russian tank; the South Vietnamese general about to pull the trigger of a pistol at the head of an adolescent Vietcong suspect; Americans pushing Vietcong suspects from helicopters to their deaths – these are all signs from battlefields that activate different myths within the overall army paradigm.

Media paradigms

We move on now to consider the medium itself as a sign that derives meaning from the way it differs from the other media in its paradigm. Thus a sign of two children leaving school could exist in one medium as a 'photograph in a family album'. That same photograph could, however, appear in another medium as a 'poster on a national safety campaign'. Here it would become less specific and more generalized. The relation between signifier and signified would change: the signifier would remain the same, but the signified would change from 'Matthew and Lucy coming home from school, July 1978', to a more generalized sign of 'children leaving school'. The more the children appear to be culturally typical on this poster (the more, that is, they exhibit what Barthes calls 'canonic generality'), the wider would be the acceptance of this new sign. Television as a medium is particularly well suited to taking a specific iconic sign like a photograph and generalizing it into a broader sign, which means giving the original sign a new level of culturally determined meaning.

Thus the very same visual image will mean slightly different things, or convey different kinds of meaning, depending on the medium through which that image is channelled. Just as there is a set or paradigm of letters from which to choose to make up words, so there is a set or paradigm of different media. An image can be presented on television or in a cinema, in a poster or a magazine, in a family photograph album or an art gallery. Television, as a 'unit' within this media paradigm, will establish its meanings in relation to other units: it emerges as more public, for instance, than the family photograph, more domestic than the poster, more casual than the art gallery.

Genre paradigms

But even within a single medium the sign will vary according to its context or *genre*. Hence a television shot of the children leaving school could, for instance, occur:

1. In a documentary film on their family: this would give it the specificity of a family photo modified by some of the generality of television.
2. In a fictional play: this would give it a different sort of specificity in that the children would be acting and not being (an additional order of signs would have been inserted), and the generality would be moved towards universality by the art of the dramatist.
3. In a safety propaganda film or an advertisement: this would de-specify the sign and refer it to the myth order of signification entirely.

So both the medium and the genre have paradigmatic attributes. The sign is different in each of the three genres above, for although the signifier remains the same, the sign itself is altered by the change of genre within the medium, in the same way as it is by a change of medium itself.

Syntagms

The units selected from the various paradigms are then combined into a meaningful whole called a *syntagm*. Syntagms, like sentences, which exist in time, are easily thought of as a chain. But syntagms of visual signs can exist simultaneously in space. Thus a sign of two children leaving school, in black silhouette, can be syntagmatically combined with a red triangle on a road sign to mean 'School: beware of children'. (We may note, incidentally, how this sign contains both arbitrary and iconic features.) Here there are only two units of meaning to be combined.

The safety poster, however, containing a photograph of the children leaving school, would be far more complex. It would contain more information, more units of meaning. Greimas (1966) uses the word *seme* to refer to the smallest units of meaning in a sign or word. The word *children*, according to his theory, is actually composed of the semes *young* and *people*, and is thus a unit in two paradigms – 'the ages of man' and 'young creatures'.

To analyse our poster as a syntagm of semes, we need first to establish the paradigm from which the poster itself is selected. This is the paradigm of signs of 'children in potentially dangerous situations' and not of 'children enjoying their holidays'. (The road sign, on the other hand, is selected from the paradigm of 'potentially dangerous situations for the motorist'.) The next task is to identify the semes, which turn out to be: two/excited/children/male and female/seven and six years old/leaving school. Each seme is itself a unit in a paradigm and derives its meaning partly from what it is not. If we change one seme, for instance if we change the ages of the children to fourteen and four, we can see what a difference would be made to the whole syntagm: it would signify a greater responsibility on the part of the older child and thus imply a less urgent need for caution from us. A full analysis of the poster would indicate the paradigms of each seme and hence the potential alternatives that were not selected. Such an analysis would look like this:

Syntagm→ two	excited	children	male and female	seven and six years old	leaving school
six	sad	adults	two males	fourteen and four	playing with fire
three	angry	teenagers	two females	eight and eight	swimming
one	sulking	babies	female and male	five and nine	climbing trees
etc.	etc.	etc.		etc.	etc.

Paradigms

Changing any one seme for another in its paradigm will change the meaning of the whole syntagm without altering the paradigm of which the poster itself is a member. This shows us the potential range of alternatives from which the photographer or advertiser has made his selection, and it is only by looking at what was rejected that we can gauge the full significance of the poster as it has finally emerged.

An analysis of a TV syntagm

To conclude this chapter, we would like to analyse a brief extract from *Cathy Come Home*, a documentary drama about the plight of the homeless in London, shown on British TV in 1966. The extract is a sequence of five shots of children in a large institutional home:

Shot 1   A close-up of a girl standing against a brick wall, looking seriously at, rather than eating, a sandwich (3 secs). Cut to

Shot 2   (*a*) A wire cage covering the stairwell of the building, the camera pans diagonally upwards following children running and laughing upstairs; (*b*) the camera is 'too close' to them, so we get blurred images of legs, bodies, faces, against the iron balustrade of the stairs (7 secs). Cut to

Shot 3 The children running, laughing along a dim corridor towards the camera, backlit (2 secs). Cut to

Shot 4 Children outside, against a brick wall, they run away from it towards the camera which zooms back to accommodate them (6 secs). Cut to

Shot 5 A child standing against a brick wall, seriously putting a bullet into a toy gun, close up, visually very similar to shot 1 (4 secs). (Total time: 22 seconds)

The iconic nature of the signs and their denotative meaning are clear, but the connotative and mythic meanings will repay closer inspection. In this 'children' syntagm, the signifiers in the denotative order become the signs in the connotative order of a crowded, constricting environment which contains but cannot dampen the resilience of the children. In the connotative order the signs express emotional attitudes. These are conveyed by camera distance, angle, the lighting effects and so on. The camera distance is close up in shots 1, 2, 4 and 5, and in 1, 4 and 5 the child is tight against a wall, constricted between camera and wall. In shot 2 the camera itself is too close, it cannot back away enough to take a 'good' picture. In shot 3 the constraint is provided by the enclosing corridor and the back lighting, which gives the impression of the children running into an enclosed environment, away from the light and freedom. The cage and iron bars of the balustrade, and the grained bricks in shots 1, 4 and 5, denote 'cultural' objects which in their turn also connote constriction.

Paradigmatic analysis requires us to compare the effect of close-up with that of long shot, of dim back lighting with that of bright front: we have to imagine how the same 'reality' could have been shot differently in order to understand why it was shot as it was. Similarly, in shot 5 for example, we can only understand the significance of the boy's gun by contrasting it with other toys he could have had, say a bubble pipe, a lump of plasticine or a fire engine. The fact that the gun is a relatively realistic one that can be loaded with 'bullets' is also significant. The child may be only playing aggression now, but the hint of real violence to follow is clearly contained in the sign.

In syntagmatic analysis, on the other hand, we relate each shot to the others. We note that shots 1 and 5 are visually similar, that they are of contemplative, still, children, who look almost cowed by the system. These 'contain' the active shots, in the way that the constricting environment contains and constrains the energy of the children. This enables us to show how the syntagm is constructed and unified, how its components affect each other, and how it operates as a coherent unit in the larger discourse of the play.

But the double order of signification is not entirely explained by reference to denotation and connotation. We have already noted that signs in the denotative order can also become, in the second order, signifiers of a myth; that is they lose their iconic specificity of reference and acquire their significance from, in this case, two culturally located myths – the myth by which we apprehend childhood as a free, unconstrained, happy experience, and the one by which we evaluate the urban and institutional environments as unnatural, constricting and hostile. The signs activate these two myth structures in the viewers, and it is their conflation that is the final significance of the signs. The second-order systems of myth and connotation support and depend on each other for they both derive from the same first-order system.

We can see how these myths and connotations are triggered, by looking more closely at the central shot of the syntagm. In this the running and laughter of the children is a *metonym* (in the first order) of happy, unrestrained childhood, it is an actual part of it. The corridor, however, is a *metaphor* in the second order (connotative), for the restrictive nature of the institution, and the way it dominates and encloses the children in it. The children are running happily away from the light into the institutional dimness, and this also is a *metaphor* in the second-order (myth), for their innocent ignorance of how their institutional childhood will blight their lives.

4 THE CODES OF TELEVISION

I N our discussion of paradigms and syntagms, we have begun to show how signs can be organized into meaningful systems, or codes. Indeed, at its simplest, a code may be defined as a 'vertical' *set* of signs (paradigm) which may be *combined* according to certain 'horizontal' *rules* (syntagm). To this very basic definition we must add the fact that the signs which comprise the set and the rules for combining them must in some way be agreed upon among the members of the culture for whom that code communicates.

Bringing the concept of code to that of the sign is bringing another dimension to our analysis of how signs work, for it focuses on the social function of the sign rather than on its structure. A code depends upon the agreement of its users. But the concept 'code' can be misleading. It may be thought to imply that a code is a static system. It may sometimes be; for instance the code by which we communicate the movement of pieces in chess is fixed and unchanging, but this is not typical. Most codes are dynamic systems, continually evolving to meet the changing needs and practices of their users. The English language, our most sophisticated code, is constantly evolving. New words are added (paradigmatic change) as are new conventions and rules by which we combine them (syntagmatic change). So in any dynamic or evolving code, there is a constant tension between tradition and innovation or between convention and originality.

It is this dynamic aspect of the code that enables it to cope with the new demands of an individual artist (e.g. James Joyce in *Finnegan's Wake*) or those of a changed cultural situation, as when the establishment of middle-class consciousness shaped the development of the novel in the late seventeenth century. Anything that a man does or makes contains encoded signs of his culture, and the way in which he does or makes it is determined to a considerable extent by his culture's conventions.

In fact, the conventional or traditional aspect of the code enables it to communicate and to convey meaning. And it is by means of these conventions that a culture establishes and maintains its identity; conventions act as cohesives in all codes, whether of language, dress, behaviour, architecture or of any cultural system.

By now, our definition of code has widened and grown more diffuse. For though it may be easy to define a code, it can be much harder to identify one in practice. Some, however, are more recognizable than others and we shall start with these. They are what we call *logical codes*.

Logical codes

We may dismiss these briefly, for they play little if any part in television. They are arbitrary and static, and depend upon an explicit and binding agreement among their users. The code of chess notation is logical, so is that of mathematics.

If a botanist wishes to describe a primrose, he will use a scientific, logical code: $\u263F \oplus K(5) \, C(5) \, A \, O + 5 \, G(5)$. This means, as Guiraud (1975) tells us: 'hermaphrodite, radial symmetry, five sepalled calyx, five petalled corolla with five attached stamens, and a five carpelled pistil, the ovaries of which are placed higher than the level at which the petals are inserted' (p. 57). This verbal translation of the formulaic code is a logical code too. A logical code, then, is totally constrained by convention, and consists of arbitrary, un-motivated signs. Verbal language has the potential to be a logical code, and scientists and lawyers, for instance, at-tempt to use it as such. But its wide range of uses means that the strict definition of meaning demanded by a logical code is rarely possible, a word must bring with it associations from elsewhere. The verbal scientific code to describe a primrose contains the word *hermaphrodite*, which, however faintly, refers us back to Hermes and Aphrodite in a way that the sign ☿ does not. Verbal language, then, has more dimen-sions; one of which we call *aesthetic*.

Aesthetic codes

Aesthetic codes tend to use more motivated signs, and to operate on both denotative and connotative levels of signifi-cation. (Logical codes avoid connotative meanings like the plague.) Further, as Guiraud (1975) says:

> The arts and literature create message-objects, which, as objects, are over and above the immediate signs which subtend them, and bearers of their own meaning, and belong to a specific semiology, that of stylization, hypo-stasis of the signifier, symbolization, etc. (p. 7)

This means that aesthetic codes differ from logical codes not in kind, but in degree. Because of their degree of motivation, aesthetic signs are less conventionalized and thus less codified than logical ones. But they *are* convention-alized nevertheless and, as we would expect, there is a correlation between the degree of conventionality and the popularity or decodability of the aesthetic construct. In general, the more conventional and constraining the code, the more popular and less highbrow is the work of art.

A new art form or style may appear meaningless at first, yet as it becomes more widely used and known, so its signs become conventionalized and thus more easily decoded.

But convention, in aesthetic codes, never imposes the constraint that it does in logical ones: it can always be broken
without a total breakdown in communication. This com-
parative freedom of art to break its own codes is explained
by Culler (1976) thus:

> aesthetic expression aims to communicate notions, subtle-
> ties, complexities which have not yet been formulated,
> and therefore, as soon as an aesthetic code comes to be
> generally perceived as a code . . . then works of art tend to
> move beyond this code. They question, parody, and
> generally undermine the code while exploring its possible
> mutations and extensions. One might even say that much
> of the interest of works of art lies in the ways in which
> they explore and modify the codes which they seem to be
> using; and this makes semiological investigation of these
> systems both highly relevant and extremely difficult. (pp.
> 100–1)

This extending or even breaking of the code is possible because the highly motivated nature of the aesthetic sign
imposes a necessary relationship between the signified and
the signifier, though we must recognize that the signified
may be and frequently is of a subjective, interior order of
reality. However, the television director does not have this
artistic freedom. He is constrained by the conventional
nature of the medium and the expectations of the audience.

These audience expectations, set by the norms of the
medium, are instrumental in the final meaning of the television 'shot'. Baggaley and Duck (1976) have shown that if
a speaker is televised in half profile, the shot tends to be
decoded as being of a more reliable and expert figure than
if the same speaker is televised full face. Television normally
shows 'expert' interviewees in half profile talking to an interviewer, whereas performers or newsreaders (who present
other people's knowledge) are shot full-face. This is a case
where the televisual code differs from that of real life, and
politicians who address the camera direct as though it were

a voter may do well to recognize this: indeed in American party political broadcasting it is now common for the politician to be interviewed, whereas in Britain he normally addresses the camera. So a television director's choice of shots is constrained by the norms already established by the medium; the art-film director will expect to establish his own norms in the film.

Codification and convention

The way these norms or conventions are established is called by Guiraud *codification*. It may be an ugly term, but it does emphasize the fact that the sorts of codes we are dealing with here are dynamic, and that codification (and decodification) of the sign is a constant process. The frequent use of a sign makes it more conventional, and extends the number of users who agree on its meaning, or, to put it another way, increases the probability that it will be decoded similarly by different receivers. Metz (1974) shows how the white hat gradually became codified into the signifier of a 'good' cowboy, but then became a cliché and lost its power. What seems to happen in this process is that at some point a sign becomes over-used, and then its receivers see its signifier as determined entirely by convention and not at all by reality: at this point it ceases to be an effective sign, and becomes a cliché.

Television, a highly conventional medium, constantly uses signs that teeter on the brink of becoming clichés. We have noted how a man in a detective drama showing the inside of his wallet is agreed to signify a plain-clothes policeman identifying himself, and not a pedlar of dirty postcards. In the same context, a sign of a man in a raincoat peering into a shop window signifies a policeman pretending not to follow or observe a particular suspect (reading a newspaper in the street is a similarly codified sign, though usually of a criminal watching). We would feel cheated if this signifier turned out to be of a mere passer-by window-shopping: the code would have been broken, our agreement shattered.

The smallest signifying unit

Identifying codes in practice is much harder than defining them in theory, particularly when we are dealing with dynamic aesthetic codes which are shaped primarily by convention or unstated agreement among the users. The issue is complicated still further by the fact that signs can belong to more than one aesthetic code, and so codes can overlap and interrelate in a network of signification, for each sign will inevitably bring with it contextual associations derived from its use in other codes. This can be consciously exploited, as when the 'voice-over' commentary commonly associated with news and documentary programmes is used to bring with it a sense of reality to a play like *Cathy Come Home*. Less deliberate, though not less significant, is the way in which signs from a code of 'the numerical evaluation of human performance' link *Come Dancing*, *Olympic Diving*, *The Generation Game* and *The Eurovision Song Contest*.

But codes not only overlap, they also operate on a number of different levels, arranged in a hierarchy. Identifying a code depends ultimately on our ability to identify its smallest signifying unit, or the base of its hierarchy. This is generally known as the *seme*, but the term has been applied particularly to visual signs. In written language, the smallest signifying unit is the letter. The letters in the paradigmatic set of the alphabet are combined syntagmatically into words, which themselves form paradigms and are combined into syntagmatic units called phrases or sentences. So we can trace the levels upwards through paragraphs and chapters, until we reach the level of books, etc., which ultimately form part of our cultural experience.

Baggaley and Duck (1976) conducted a series of experiments to ascertain the effect of certain semes in a television shot. A speaker was televised by two cameras simultaneously: the only difference was that camera 1 showed the notes to which he was referring, while in the shot from camera 2, his eyes as he paused were directed apparently at nothing. Audience reaction showed that the presence of notes in the shot made the speaker seem significantly less fair and more confusing. In another experiment, a speaker was shown either against a curtain or against an appropriate photograph. The photograph background did not, as might be supposed, make him more interesting, but did make him appear more profound, more reliable and more fair; in other words it raised his credibility and increased the amount of trust the viewers were prepared to invest in him. The variation of a seme clearly affected the semantics of the shot. Whether the seme is in a real-life or specifically tele-visual code is much harder to decide, but it does appear that 'lecture notes' as a seme has a different meaning on tele-vision from its meaning in reality. It may well be that the expert speaker on television uses an autocue, and thus 'lecture notes', by convention or usage, becomes the sign of an amateur, as in *Open Door* or other access programmes. Or they may signify the reporter on the spot who has not had time to write a 'proper' report; in both cases the seme would be in a televisual code. On the other hand, we could argue that a speaker looking into nothing is giving us a sign that he is marshalling his thoughts: in this case the meaning would be located in real-life codes. In practice, as the two interpretations are congruent, we probably respond to both.

Codes and perception

This quest for the smallest signifying unit of the code is important, for it helps us to establish where real life ends and television begins – a boundary that is not as clearly drawn as it might appear to be at first sight. This boundary is blurred because the way we watch television and the way we perceive reality are fundamentally similar, in that both are determined by conventions or codes. Reality is itself a complex system of signs interpreted by members of the cul-ture in exactly the same way as are films or television pro-grammes. Perception of this reality is always mediated through the codes with which our culture organizes it, categorizes its significant elements or semes into paradigms, and relates them significantly into syntagms. Our response to nature is codified, and our perception of a sunset, a stag-beetle or a man's eye movements relies on an encoding and decoding process that is as specific to our culture as our language is. The signified is as arbitrary as the signifier, because its form is culturally determined.

Art claims to be able to make us see familiar things in a new way, and this newness resides in the opposition between the newly created aesthetic code and our normal code of perception. In practice, of course, no aesthetic code can be entirely specific to the work of art within which it operates; it must relate to other works in the same school. Television is, however, a more conventional medium than art-film in the sense that its codes relate more closely to the normal codes of perception. It is this that gives it its position of cultural centrality, and that makes the boundary between television and reality difficult to define.

Thus the distinction between televisual and real-life codes is blurred on all levels but the technical; indeed the relationship between the two is a dynamic one in which each affects the other. Knightley (1975) describes how American GIs in Vietnam acted out conventional 'war movies' when they saw the CBS newsreel cameras arrive. The cameras then photographed them doing this and so the viewer at home saw what he thought was a real code of be-haviour (i.e. one dictated by the demands of the situation), though it was in fact derived from a fictional code, itself a signifier of the real one. An interesting consequence of this is that the viewer would presumably find the realism of the war movies validated by the television newsreel. This is a particularly explicit example of the interrelationship be-tween real and fictional codes, or direct perceptual codes and mediated ones, but the interrelationship is always there, even in subtler, less explicit forms.

In short, television is one kind of reality, and the culture to which we belong is another. But we perceive both of them in a similar way, and as a result they interact with each other. Furthermore, watching television shares with everyday life the characteristic of being a familiar and casual activity which most of us engage in without feeling the need for elaborate analysis. But as Lévi-Strauss (1973) has suggested, 'understanding consists in reducing one type of reality to another' (p. 70). Television 'reduces' cultural experience to another (no less valid) form of reality. Following in its wake, we have attempted in these chapters to 'reduce' television itself to another type of reality; that of a semiotic system of signs and codes. The current unfamiliarity of semiotics makes our reduction quite obvious, whereas that of television is more self-effacing. However, just as semiotic analysis puts the television experience at a distance in order to 'read' it, so too can reading the television message provide us with a view of larger cultural processes. In the next chapters we shall pursue some of the more important ways in which television interacts with our culture. As a result we hope to construct a set of square-eyed spectacles, as it were, through which we can 'read' that culture itself.

5 THE FUNCTIONS OF TELEVISION

Just as all living organisms live in certain specialized environments to which they adapt and which completely determine their lives, so do human beings live, to a significant extent, in an ocean of words. The difference is that the human environment is, to a large extent, man made. We secrete words into the environment around us just as we secrete carbon dioxide and, in doing so, we create an invisible semantic environment of words which is part of our existence in quite as important ways as the physical environment. The content of verbal output does not merely passively reflect the complex social, political, and economic reality of the human race: it interacts with it as well. As our semantic environment incorporates the verbal outputs secreted into it, it becomes both enriched and polluted, and these changes are largely responsible for the course of human history. (Rapoport 1969, p. 36)

RAPOPORT'S thought-provoking metaphor suggests that we both create and are sustained by our language. We are, in other words, produced by the environment of signification that we have collectively produced. Part of that environment comprises the constant stream of 'secretions' that emanate from the small screen.

However, we cannot merely 'ingest' those secretions, any more than we can merely ingest food. Just as our metabolic processes transform what we eat into material that can be assimilated, so our culturally learnt codes and conventions transform what we watch from mere external stimuli into actual *communication*, where the message is not only received but also decoded, understood and responded to.

Moreover, as Rapoport's metaphor indicates, the codes and conventions which comprise our particular culture's ways of seeing are incorporated into the modes of perception of each individual to such an extent that we are largely unconscious of their operation, just as we have little consciousness of, or control over, our metabolic processes when we digest food. Our perception is not so much an inherited mechanism as a learnt one – the daily manifestation of our whole personal history of socialization and interaction with the cultural environment. Hence the awareness we bring to the television screen is a precondition for making sense of what we see, but that awareness is itself produced in us by what we have experienced hitherto.

Of course it is often difficult in practice to bear this complex relationship in mind. After all, television is literally a highly visible medium, and it does seem to influence people's behaviour, if only to the extent that more people watch for more hours today than they did a generation ago. It is a short step from this observation to one which proposes that television, unaided, *causes* people to sit and watch. It comes in some quarters to be regarded as a pest. It has the same kind of reputation as a fox who gets into a chicken coop and kills indiscriminately far more chickens than it could possibly eat or drag away. Clearly the fox is a menace and one of nature's deviants. However, in the heat of the moment it is easy to forget that the fox exhibits this wanton behaviour not through natural malice. On the contrary, his behaviour is conditioned by the environment which the farmer has created, whereby more chickens than would naturally congregate together are cooped up with no means of escape. The 'historical circumstances' governing the lives of the chickens are the cause of their downfall, not the fox. But the onlooker finds it convenient to blame the innate brutality of the predator, and not the farmer's culturally determined method of keeping chickens.

Similarly, television is often blamed not so much for killing chickens – or even viewers – but certainly for producing results which are in fact conditioned by much broader and more diffuse historical circumstances. Even the number of hours people spend watching television is not ultimately caused by television itself. It results, much more obviously, from shorter working hours, increased family resources available for leisure, and from the likelihood that in many cases the hours television fills were previously filled by various activities, like knitting, chatting or even dozing, with which the new medium seems to be able to co-exist quite comfortably. It has brought new stimulus into the home, and created a demand for more rather than less entertainment of other kinds. More books, magazines and newspapers are read, more music heard, and more plays and films are seen now than ever before – even if 'only' on television. It brings a good many of these competitors into the living rooms of families who would otherwise be deprived of them. The fox, in short, has become the farmer.

The functional tradition

Looking at television from a semiotic and cultural perspective is, however, not the oldest and perhaps not the most respectable academic approach to the medium. That honour belongs to the sociology of mass communications, which grew up largely in the USA where academic interest in television's predecessor in the mass communications field, the press, had always been high.

This tradition has in fact shaped the way most of us think about television, especially in relation to the questions we are pursuing in this chapter; namely the relationship between the television message, the everyday reality of the audience, and the functions performed by television for that audience.

We speak here of an academic tradition because, although many of the early theories about television's effect on its audience have been modified, extended or discredited, it remains the case that later research has built upon and not entirely supplanted the assumptions inherent in the early work. For this reason, it is necessary to be aware of the most important of those underlying assumptions. There are at least three, which can best be thought of under the following headings: (1) individualism; (2) abstraction; and (3) functionalism.

1 *Individualism*

This assumption presupposes a one-to-one relationship between the mass communicator and the individual viewer which is justified by reference to the one-to-one model of face-to-face communication. From this assumption, which leaves out of account the fact that much of an individual's response is culturally determined and not internally motivated, has grown the habit of regarding the television viewer as an individual with certain psychological needs. He takes these needs with him to the television screen, and the mass communicator attempts to gratify them. Hence television is seen as a 'need-gratification' medium.

2 *Abstraction*

Here the assumption is that an individual's psychological needs are much the same no matter what society or culture he belongs to. Certainly a man's culture can be included as one of the factors which influence these needs, but nevertheless the basic notions imply a kind of universality and timelessness about human relations, which derive no doubt from humanist myths about the existence of a universal 'human nature'. As a result, this approach tends to disregard the historical processes which have produced such formative developments as the division of labour, class oppositions, regional cultures, economic differentials and the various subcultures, in favour of general psychological needs.

3 Functionalism

This approach assumes that television is used by its viewers to satisfy their psychological needs, in a more or less conscious and active way. Functional analysis concentrates on the relations between the different parts in a system, in order to discover how they work and the functions they perform. In respect of television the relationships between the (individual) viewer, the communicator, the channels used and such external factors from the social and cultural experience of the viewer as can be identified (or better still quantified), are all described in terms of their effect upon each other. The notion of functionalism derives from a well-established sociological discipline, and in the field of mass communication it has extended the range of the earlier stimulus-response assumptions. The most recent research has developed from this into what is called the 'uses and gratifications' theory.

Uses and gratifications

We can now refer to some of the specific needs posited by sociologists of mass communication. These needs are always derived ultimately from the individual psyche. Katz *et al.* (1973) list five basic needs to be fulfilled by the mass media. They are:

1 Cognitive needs: the acquiring of information, knowledge and understanding.
2 Affective needs: the need for emotional and aesthetic experience, love and friendship; the desire to see beautiful things.

3 Personal integrative needs: the need for self-confidence, stability, status, reassurance.
4 Social integrative needs: the need for strengthening contacts with family, friends and others.
5 Tension-release needs: the need for escape and diversion.

Similarly De Fleur and Ball-Rokeach (1975) propose an 'integrated theory' of mass media effects, in which the idea of needs becomes the basis for understanding the media as a whole. Their three categories of need are:

1 The need to understand one's social world.
2 The need to act meaningfully and effectively in that world.
3 The need for fantasy-escape from daily problems and tensions.

These needs supply the basis for De Fleur and Ball-Rokeach's 'dependency theory', which is taken to indicate that everyone in modern urban industrialized western society is psychologically dependent to a great extent on the mass media for information which enables them to enter into full participation in society.

One of the most striking examples of the application of this approach came in the study by Peled and Katz (1974) of the media functions in Israel during the war of 1973. Not surprisingly, they found that 'dependence' on the mass media tended to increase in a society in crisis. In this situation, individuals' expectations for 'information and interpretation' from the media were in fact largely supplied by them. The audience were described as 'active' in the sense that they turned to the media with explicit expectations. However, Peled and Katz assert that the 'manifest analysis of message content' (into categories like news, entertainment, etc.) is not necessarily sufficient to predict the use to which that content will be put. Especially in the case of television, the messages served not merely the need for information but also the 'need for relief from tension and for a feeling of social connectedness'.

The hypodermic needle

Clearly the individualist–functionalist view of television does take account of the context within which the television message becomes meaningful. But it also tends to assimilate that context as one of the given variables in a highly predictable set of influences on the individual. Hence any breakdown in the flow of communication from the mass communicator to the individual is as often as not seen as a kind of 'dysfunction' operating to the detriment of the individual's personal satisfaction. Wright (1964) discusses such dysfunctions in relation to the gratification of the individual's need for surveillance of his society – a need usually seen as being gratified by the provision of quantities of news. But news itself, says Wright, might be dysfunctional: 'For example, large amounts of raw news may overwhelm him and lead to personal anxiety, apathy, or other reactions which would interfere with his reception of the items of news about the environment necessary for his normal operations' (p. 107).

Indeed, for Wright, even 'handling' (editing) the 'large amounts of raw news' might still leave the individual operative in a dysfunctional state, since the news itself 'sometimes increases personal tensions and anxiety which, in turn, leads the individual to reduce his attention to the news (hence disturbing the normal state of equilibrium)'. For Wright, then, it is appropriate that the bread of news should be leavened by the judicious addition of quantities of entertainment. The function of entertainment, in its turn, is 'to provide respite for the individual which, perhaps, permits him to continue to be exposed to the mass-communicated news, interpretation, and prescriptions so necessary for his survival in the modern world' (p. 108).

The language used by Wright is illuminating. He seems

to imagine the individual viewer of television as a mechanism whose needs are merely those of equilibrium-maintenance and continued 'exposure' to the 'necessary' doses of news. Entertainment is merely an anodyne, rather than a positive characteristic of television in its own right. This is in fact a classic statement of the 'hypodermic needle' model (sometimes also called the 'bullet theory') of mass communication's uses and effects. Wright himself has modified this stance in more recent studies (Wright 1975), during the course of which he has given a succinct summary of the hypodermic needle model. It is derived, he notes, from the equally simplistic notion of the audience as a mere 'mass'. As a mass, an audience displays the following four characteristics:

1 It comprises people from all walks of life.
2 It comprises anonymous individuals.
3 Its members share little experience with each other – there is little interaction between them.
4 Its members are disunited – they are very loosely organized.

Wright comments:

> Usually accompanying this concept of a mass audience is an image of the communications media as acting directly upon individual audience members – reaching each member or not, influencing him or her directly or not. This view of mass communications has been called the 'hypodermic needle model': each audience member in the mass audience is personally and directly 'stuck' by the medium's message. Once the message has stuck someone, it may or may not have the influence, depending on whether or not it is potent enough to 'take'. (1975, p. 79)

The modification Wright proposes to this simple model is one whereby 'a conception of the audience has emerged in which greater notice is taken of the social context within which each audience member operates'. But here again the context is seen merely as a variable, rather than a funda-mental determinant of the process of communication.

One of the most striking results of the approach we have been describing can be observed in its attitude to individuals who for whatever reason are under-exposed to media in-fluences. They come to be regarded as sufferers from a new kind of social malady, namely 'media-deprivation'. This notion requires that we define the media primarily in terms of their function of disseminating news and public affairs from an informed elite to a dependent mass public. It ignores both the use to which that public might put any given message, and the fact that people who choose not to watch the news are capable of leading relatively normal and fulfilled lives. Hence this approach can be seen as a mani-festation of the same ideology which, in the 1960s especially, discovered 'verbal deprivation' and 'cultural deprivation' in all social groups other than the educated elite. This ideology impinged on the world of practical politics through the at-tempts that were made to rectify these cultural deficiencies with educational 'programmes of intervention'. (For a good analysis of the 'cultural deprivation' debate, see Open University 1972.)

Notice also that this kind of sociological analysis of the mass media's relation with our culture does not seek to go beyond an account of opinions and attitudes of individual people. In this sense television can no doubt have an in-fluence, but it is worth remembering that the opinions and attitudes of most people are chosen from a set which is circumscribed very largely by the modes of thought, the ways of seeing which a culture negotiates for itself. Tele-vision cannot easily step outside this central set of choices, and if it did its influence would no doubt be marginal.

Mass consumption or mass communication?

In fact much previous research into the relationship of mass communication with its audience has been more interested in its 'massness' than in its efficacy as communication. Part of the reason for this has been the inevitable feedback into sociological research of data and assumptions deriving from research done by the broadcasting institutions or their agencies (Neilsen for instance in the USA, JICTAR and BBC Audience Research in the UK).

This kind of research has led to a commonly held view of the audience which has at least coloured the findings of numerous academic inquiries over the years; namely the definition of the audience as a 'market', comprising people whose shared characteristic is that they are all 'consumers' of television output. McQuail (1975) has pointed to the contradiction in this definition:

> Audience research, as usually conducted, is a form of market research and hence represents the audience as market – a body of consumers of a particular product. We do not normally regard the recipients of communication in other contexts in this way: the people we talk to are not 'consumers' of our words, children are not a market for their lessons, employees of an organisation are not consumers of organisational messages, nor are voters a market for the appeals of political leaders. (pp. 187f.)

Naturally, the broadcasting institutions themselves are locked into the prevailing market economy, and it is perhaps tempting for their executives to think in terms of moving a 'product' to a 'market'. But this language is of course metaphorical; audiences do not 'buy' television messages, and they do not 'consume' the messages transmitted to them.

Hence in order to understand their relationship to the medium, and the effect or otherwise of that medium in their lives, we must concentrate on the dimension which market-oriented research at least most often ignores: the fact that television is *communication* as well as *mass*. As McQuail suggests:

> ... the problem in obtaining or interpreting evidence about effects in general lies partly in the inappropriateness of many formulations of the process of mass communication, a failure to acknowledge that this is a subtle and complex process, a matter of bargaining, interaction and exchange just as much as a conversation is between two people. (p. 191)

Clearly an approach which is based on the communicative characteristics of 'bargaining, interaction and exchange' (not to mention the negotiation of meaning) will be interested not merely in the number, purchasing power, socioeconomic status or opinions and attitudes of the audience. Such an approach must also take into account the way in which the members of the audience communicate with each other, and the elements which go to make up an act of communication. Since communication is essentially interpersonal and not intrapersonal, a psychological approach can have only a limited relevance to the study of communication. We can recognize that even though an individual's psychological motivation does mediate his behaviour, that behaviour is normally oriented towards the external world rather than to his internal mental state (see Elliott 1974).

If the mass media are to influence individuals, then, as a form of communication, they must do so according to the rules of communication in general. How does any communication actually influence the receiver of a message? McQuail has isolated five conditions, while stressing that

> ... the central and universal feature of communication influence is the voluntary compliance of the receiver to the sender. The relationship between them is a power relationship ... The forms of compliance are diverse, and social situations are usually too complex to find a one-to-

one relationship between a type of power and a given case of influence. (p. 163)

The five general conditions which bear upon the effect of communication are:

1 The greater the monopoly of the communication source over the recipient, the greater the change or effect in favour of the source over the recipient.

2 Communication effects are greatest where the message is in line with the existing opinions, beliefs and dispositions of the receiver.

3 Communication can produce the most effective shifts on unfamiliar, lightly felt, peripheral issues, which do not lie at the centre of the recipient's value systems.

4 Communication is more likely to be effective where the source is believed to have expertise, high status, objectivity or likeability, but particularly where the source has power, and can be identified with.

5 The social context, group or reference group will mediate the communication and influence whether or not it is accepted. (pp. 157–63)

As a result, we can expect the direct effect of *mass* communication upon individual's behaviour and attitudes to be precisely as McQuail suggests: 'either non-existent, very small, or beyond measurement by current techniques' (p. 191). Beyond this lame and impotent conclusion the most we can expect of the mass media is that they can provide 'frames of reference' and 'cognitive detail' about the world: the famous 'agenda-setting' effect of the media which can supply for the different audience groups 'a quite uniformly held and specific "definition of the situation" ' (p. 192). Of course, any definition of the situation which can be supplied under the five conditions noted above and still tend to 'override personal experience', must communicate a message that is very close to the culture's collective centre, one which people can accept in the knowledge that it derives from deeply held and widely diffused ways of interpreting the world.

If mass communication is indeed communication, then it must communicate something. McQuail *et al.* (1972) have classified under four headings the relationship of media content (what it says) to audience use (what we do with it). They suggest that this relationship has to do with:

1 Diversion
   (*a*) escape from the constraints of routine
   (*b*) escape from the burdens of problems
   (*c*) emotional release
2 Personal relationships
   (*a*) companionship
   (*b*) social utility
3 Personal identity
   (*a*) personal reference
   (*b*) reality exploration
   (*c*) value reinforcement
4 Surveillance – maintaining an overall view of the immediate environment. (p. 155)

It is interesting that this classification was erected partly in response to the inadequacy of previous theories, which had overstressed the escapist function of television. And yet the idea of television communication providing escape is still firmly embedded in the Diversion category.

But escape is not just a matter of the inhabitants of Jubilee Close watching *Coronation Street*, though that kind of self-reflexive escape is indeed popular. It is important to remember that the 'bargaining, interaction and exchange' of the communication process *itself* functions as part of the entertainment, bonding us as viewers, via the message, to the reality of our culture, and thus lifting the burden of an isolating individualism from our shoulders. This is not the kind of gratification, however, that is easy to articulate for social scientists' questionnaires. It's easier to say that 'TV takes you out of yourself'.

Who is the communicator?

If the relationship of the audience to the communicated message is a peculiarly complex one, then so is the relationship of the audience to the communicator. To begin with, analysts of mass communication are faced with an apparent paradox which does not occur in most other forms of communication. Neither party in the communication act knows who the other is. Normally when one party encodes a message according to one set of codes and conventions and a second party decodes that message according to different codes, the result is known as an *aberrant decoding*. For example, the masons and glaziers who built Chartres Cathedral constructed their statues and windows to communicate to the members of their well-defined and relatively cohesive culture their sense of man's place in relation to time, God and the revelations of the testaments, by means of certain familiar sacred stories told in stone and glass. The modern perceiver of these same messages may well decode them as perfect examples of gothic art, or as manifestations of the medieval delight in resemblances, numerology, etc. The modern decoding is *aberrant* in relation to the communicative intentions of the encoder. The cultural context of the two parties is different.

As Eco (1972, pp. 104–6) has pointed out, aberrant decoding is quite normal in the field of the mass media. Logically this must be the case since the professional encoders and the 'undifferentiated mass of receivers', respectively, cannot be certain in a complex society like ours that they speak the same language (see Smith 1973, pp. 49–50). However, this very characteristic of the television communication imposes a discipline on the encoders which ensures that their messages are in touch with the central meaning systems of the culture, and that the codes in which the message is transmitted are widely available. The very possibility that the audience might use the message in ways not intended by the encoder has a double effect: it drives the professionals towards the centre of their culture (just as the masons and glaziers of Chartres used their plastic and visual media to communicate messages already very familiar in their culture); and, conversely, it protects the audience members from direct coercion or even influence towards any particular version of the truth. (We shall pursue the implications of the latter effect in more detail in chapter 8.)

A further complexity we face in understanding the communicator's relation to the audience is the problem of identifying just who 'he' is. In fact we can identify three simultaneous levels in the presentation of the communicator. They are:

1 The image on the screen, whether that image be one of a newscaster, the actors in a fictional representation, or camera shots of the world out-there – urban streetscapes, for instance.
2 The broadcasting institution, its employees and professional codes (which Smith 1973, p. 5, has called the 'ideology' of 'objectivity' or 'impartiality').
3 The culture for which the messages are meaningful. At this level the communicator is the macro-group, of many millions of people, of which each member of the audience group is a differentiated part.

Hence we can say that a culture communicates *with itself* via the mediation of the (second level) professional communicators who are manifested as the (first level) encoded messages on the screen. It follows that the television medium is not a closed system, obeying its own internal rules and relatively uninfluenced by 'external' conditions. As Hall (1973) has pointed out, the professional communicators themselves are not insulated from cultural influences. The people who are responsible for what we call 'production' of output mediate the messages but they do not *originate* them. They 'draw topics, treatments, agendas, events, personnel, images of the audience, "definitions of the situation" from the wider socio-cultural and political system, and so they cannot constitute a "closed system" ' (p. 3).

Thus we can say that there is no single 'authorial' identity for the television communicator. Furthermore, the image on the screen would hardly be able to make itself understood at all were it unable to rely upon the resources of everyday verbal language. After all, most heads on television are 'talking heads'. For this reason it is perhaps instructive to remind ourselves that television's functions are to some extent dependent upon and defined by the functions performed by speech in general. Of course, television is a semiotic system going beyond mere words – but much of its visual content takes the form of 'paralinguistic' signs derived ultimately from pre-televisual (real-life) linguistic codes. We have argued in this chapter that television functions in society as a form of communication. But the language upon which its codes are modelled itself performs several discrete functions. The linguist Jakobson (1958) has isolated six of them, all of which can be observed at work on television; indeed many of its messages seem to serve little purpose other than to perform them. Briefly, they are as follows:

1 *The referential function.* Language's most familiar function, where the relationship between a sign and its *referent* or object is dominant.
2 *The emotive function.* This concerns the relationship between a sign and its *encoder*; it expresses his attitude towards the subject of the message (e.g. 'it's been a long day' communicates the speaker's attitude towards the day, and does not refer to its time-span).
3 *The conative function.* This concerns the relationship between the sign and its *decoder*. Imperative commands are messages where the conative function is most clearly dominant.
4 *The poetic function.* Here the dominant function is the message's concern with *itself*. It is not confined to

poetry. Slogans can use it (e.g. 'I like Ike'), and so can proverbial sayings (e.g. 'Finders, keepers, losers, weepers'). It is dominant in many television advertisements.

5 *The phatic function.* Here the dominant function of the message is to stress the *act of communication* between the parties involved. Remarks about the weather are its classic example. Television programmes use it frequently; perhaps because of, rather than in spite of, the 'remote' relationship between broadcaster and viewer.

6 *The metalinguistic function.* Here the function of language is to communicate a message *about language*. Literary criticism is all metalanguage, and many television programmes, especially comedies, are 'about' the television message. Parodies like *Monty Python*, *Rutland Weekend Television*, etc., are especially adept at exploiting metalanguage, but *The Generation Game* does it too, as we shall see.

6 BARDIC TELEVISION

A T this stage we are ready to revise some of the models of television's function that were described in the last chapter. The internal psychological state of the individual is not the prime determinant in the communication of television messages. These are decoded according to individually learnt but culturally generated codes and conventions, which of course impose similar constraints of perception on the encoders of the messages. It seems, then, that television functions as a social ritual, overriding individual distinctions, in which our culture engages in order to communicate with its collective self (see Leach 1976, p. 45).

To encompass this notion, which requires that we concentrate on the messages and their language as much as on the institutions that produce them, and on the audience response as much as on the communicator's intentions, we have coined the idea of television as our own culture's *bard*. Television performs a 'bardic function' for the culture at large and all the individually differentiated people who live in it. When we use the term *bard* it is to stress certain qualities common both to this multi-originated message and to more traditional bardic utterances. First, for example, the classically conceived bard functions as a *mediator of language*, one who composes out of the available linguistic resources of the culture a series of consciously structured messages which serve to communicate to the members of that culture a confirming, reinforcing version of themselves. The traditional bard rendered the central concerns of his day into verse. We must remember that television renders our own everyday perceptions into an equally specialized, but less formal, language system.

Second, the structure of those messages is organized according to the needs of the *culture* for whose ears and eyes they are intended, and not according to the internal demands of the 'text', nor of the individual communicator. Indeed the notion of an individual author producing 'his' text is a product of literate culture. Barthes (1977) comments: 'In ethnographic societies the responsibility for a narrative is never assumed by a person but by a mediator, shaman or relator whose "performance" – the mastery of the narrative code – may possibly be admired but never his "genius". The author is a modern figure, a product of our society insofar as . . . it discovered the prestige of the individual' (pp. 142–3). The real 'authority' for both bardic and television messages is the audience in whose language they are encoded.

Third, the bardic mediator occupies the *centre* of its culture; television is one of the most highly centralized institutions in modern society. This is not only a result of commercial monopoly or government control, it is also a response to the culture's felt need for a common centre, to which the television message always refers. Its centralization speaks to all members of our highly fragmented society.

Fourth, the bardic voice is *oral*, not literate, providing a kind of cementing or compensatory discourse for a culture which otherwise places an enormous investment in the abstract, elaborated codes of literacy. These literate codes themselves provide a vast and wide-ranging – but easily avoided – cultural repertoire not appropriate to transmission by television.

Fifth, the bardic role is normally a positive and dynamic one. It is to draw into its own central position both the audience with which it communicates and the reality to which it refers. We have tried to articulate this positive role by means of the term *claw back*. The bardic mediator constantly strives to claw back into a central focus the subject of its messages. This inevitably means that some features of the subject are emphasized rather than others. For example, nature programmes will often stress the 'like us-ness' of the animals filmed, finding in their behaviour metaphoric equivalences with our own culture's way of organizing its affairs. It is this very characteristic of claw back that enables the converse function also to be performed. If a subject *cannot* be clawed back into a socio-central position the audience is left with the conclusion that some point in their culture's response to reality is inadequate. The effect is to show, by means of this observed inadequacy, that some modification in attitudes or ideology will be required to meet the changed circumstances.

Sixth, the bardic function, appropriately, has to do with *myths* (in the Bartheian sense explained in chapter 3). These are selected and combined into sequences that we have called *mythologies*. Since mythologies operate at the level of latent as opposed to manifest content, of connotation as opposed to denotation, their articulation does not have to be consciously apprehended by the viewer in order to have been successfully communicated.

In fact, mythologies can often be thought of in terms of a seventh characteristic shared by bardic television utterances and more traditional ones. They emerge as the *conventions* of seeing and knowing, the *a priori* assumptions about the nature of reality which most of the time a culture is content to leave unstated and unchallenged. It is in respect of this characteristic of its messages that we described the television medium as conventional earlier.

As Williams (1975) has pointed out in a slightly different context, conventions of this kind are not abstract, 'they are profoundly worked and reworked in our actual living relationships. They are our ways of seeing and knowing,

which every day we put into practice, and while the conventions hold, while the relationships hold, most practice confirms them' (pp. 15–16). Our 'actual living relationships'
are largely those which function through language, which
are directed outside our 'selves', and which we establish as
members of a particular culture. One of the most potent
vehicles by which these organizing conventions are 'profoundly worked and reworked' is of course the television
medium.

We suggest that the function performed by the television
medium in its bardic role can be summarized as follows:

1 To *articulate* the main lines of the established cultural
consensus about the nature of reality (and therefore the
reality of nature).

2 To *implicate* the individual members of the culture into
its dominant value-systems, by exchanging a status-
enhancing message for the endorsement of that message's underlying ideology (as articulated in its
mythology).

3 To *celebrate*, explain, interpret and justify the doings of
the culture's individual representatives in the world
out-there; using the mythology of individuality to claw
back such individuals from any mere eccentricity to a
position of socio-centrality.

4 To *assure* the culture at large of its practical adequacy
in the world by affirming and confirming its ideologies/
mythologies in active engagement with the practical
and potentially unpredictable world.

5 To *expose*, conversely, any practical inadequacies in the
culture's sense of itself which might result from changed
conditions in the world out-there, or from pressure
within the culture for a reorientation in favour of a
new ideological stance.

6 To *convince* the audience that their status and identity as
individuals is guaranteed by the culture as a whole.

7 To *transmit* by these means a sense of cultural membership (security and involvement).

These seven functions are performed in all message sequences of the television discourse; successful *communication* takes place when the members of the audience 'negotiate' their response to these functions with reference to their own peculiar circumstances. Just as the message is multi-originated, so the audience response is 'multi-conscious' – it apprehends the various levels and orders of the discourse simultaneously and without confusion (see Bethell 1944, p. 29).

However, television's colossal output in fact only represents a selection from the more prolific utterances of language in general within our culture, and thus bears a metonymic relationship to that language. As a result its messages tend to assume the further characteristic that we have stressed, namely that of *socio-centrality*. The bardic mediator tends to articulate the negotiated central concerns of its culture, with only limited and often over-mediated references to the ideologies, beliefs, habits of thought and definitions of the situation which obtain in groups which are for one reason or another peripheral. Since one of the characteristics of western culture is that the societies concerned are class-divided, television responds with a predominance of messages which propagate and re-present the dominant class ideology. Groups which can be recognized as having a culturally validated but subordinate identity, such as the young, blacks, women, rock-music fans, etc., will receive a greater or lesser amount of coverage according to their approximation to the mythology of the bourgeois.

Ritual condensation

In anthropological terms this bardic function of the television medium corresponds to what is called *ritual condensation*. Ritual condensation is the result of projecting abstract ideas (good/bad) in manifest form on to the external world (where good/bad becomes white/black). Leach (1976, pp. 37–41) explains the process:

By converting ideas, products of the mind (mentifacts), into material objects 'out-there', we give them relative permanence, and in that permanent material form we can subject them to technical operations which are beyond the capacity of the mind acting by itself. It is the difference between carrying out mathematical calculations 'in your head' and working things out with pencil and paper or on a calculating machine. (p. 37)

The projection of abstract ideas into material form is evident in such social activities as religious ritual. But the television medium also performs a similar function, when, for example, a programme like *Ironside* converts abstract ideas about individual relationships between man and man, men and women, individuals and institutions, whites and blacks into concrete dramatic form. It is a ritual condensation of the dominant criteria for survival in modern complex society. Clearly in this condensed form individual relationships can be scrutinized by the society concerned, and any inappropriateness can be dealt with in the form of criticisms of the programme. Hence *Ironside*'s ritual condensation of relationships is supplanted by *Kojak*'s, which is supplanted in turn by *Starsky and Hutch*. Each of these fictive police series presents a slightly different view of the appropriate way of behaving towards other people, and for a society which finds Starsky's boyish and physical friendship with Hutch appropriate, the paternal common sense of Ironside will emerge as old-fashioned.

The bardic function of ritual condensation occurs at what we have called the third order of signification, where the second-order myths cohere into sets or mythologies. To illustrate how this whole process manifests itself in the course of a single programme, let us return to our *News at Ten* bulletin, broadcast in January 1976.

We have noted briefly (p. 46) how the mythology of the news can be discerned as an organizing principle beneath the first and second orders. In response, the myths appealed to in the second order cohere into two main categories: there are myths activated in this bulletin which deal with our apprehension of the macro-social or *secondary* social groups – institutional units such as the army, the government, the Department of Health, local authorities, trade unions. And there are myths dealing with *primary* social groups – the individual and domestic plane of the family, personal relationships and individual behaviour. The relationships of the myths within each group, and particularly those between groups, set up a complex array of meanings at this third, ideological, order of signification, and it is in these relationships that we find the structure of the news – the form taken by its 'conceptual movement'.

Indeed, the relationship between the two main groups of myth is perceived as contradiction. The institutional mythology is presented in such a way as to produce a negative response in the audience: the mythology of the institutions is that although they are capable of decision, action, even glamour, they are at last ineffectual. Conversely, the mythology of individuals is presented in such a way as to affirm and confirm the primacy and adequacy of individual actions and relationships even when these may be operating on behalf of institutions. A man can be presented as adequate, even when he is a soldier in an army that is presented as inadequate and unable (ultimately) to cope.

However, there is an obvious sense in which a national news programme must deal more extensively with institutions than with individuals. Individuals are generally presented as functions of their institutional status. There is thus a constant dialectical interaction between the two mythologies, whose contradictions generate a tension which needs to be resolved, and to which we shall return.

Here is the news

The news opens with Andrew Gardner, the newsreader, reporting a government decision to send an army group –

the Special Air Service (SAS) – to resolve a macro-social problem in Northern Ireland. Peter Snow, the ITN defence correspondent, immediately personalizes the move:

Mr Wilson is taking a carefully calculated risk . . .

This is not merely because elite individuals can be metonymically representative of lesser mortals (see Galtang and Ruge 1973, p. 66), but also because the journalistic code takes account of the primacy of individuals, thus responding to and reaffirming the dialectic of the mythologies: what happens out-there is only a large-scale version of a generally available personal experience – a game of skill.

However, Snow's main task is to establish an identity for the then relatively unknown SAS, whose reality is in fact far from central to our culture, for it embodies many of the values that we consciously disown. But, says Snow, Mr Wilson is

putting into South Armagh the men who have the reputation, earned behind enemy lines in Indonesia, Malaya and other recent wars, for individual toughness, resourcefulness and endurance. They've been, not entirely of their own choosing, the undercover men. The men whose presence has struck fear into the heart of the enemy.

The institution (the SAS) is defined in terms of the men, whose toughness, resourcefulness and endurance is *individual*. Furthermore, as a myth, the 'reputation earned behind enemy lines' is common to many a movie or paperback: the commando/marine/'True Brit'/*Guns of Navarone*/*Green Berets* myth. Here all that changes is the signifier for this well-known myth. The SAS is now made to signify it, even though the notion of 'enemy lines' is devoid of meaning in the Northern Ireland context.

Mr Wilson, on behalf of the government, plays his game of skill by weighing up the mythic qualities and their likely effect, against what Snow calls the political 'risk'. When Snow comes to describe what the SAS will do, we are, as it were, taken behind the scenes at Battalion HQ, and initiated into the logistical minutiae of detailed planning:

In the next day or two, probably a small group, maybe half a dozen, will fly across to Armagh to have a hard long look at the ground. Another small group will join one of the army regiments to liaise with them and watch how they go about their patrolling. All this will be reported back to SAS headquarters in Hereford, where a special squad of about fifty men – very much fewer than the whole of the SAS – will have been doing a period of intensive anti-IRA training. As soon as they're ready, they'll fly to Ulster. They'll be in full uniform, not disguised as civilians. That means SAS sand-coloured berets, camouflage jackets, with perhaps a glimpse of those SAS parachute wings that every one of them wears. They'll be working in groups of four; a leader in his mid-thirties, a radio operator, a medical expert and an explosives expert. They'll be operating in the countryside, not the towns, gathering intelligence by hiding up for long periods – they can last for weeks in one place on starvation rations – and laying ambushes near the border if necessary. They'll be gathering the information and then acting on it.

We are bombarded with very precise information about the SAS, even to the age of their squad leaders. An effect of busyness and purpose is thus created. But at the same time, the object of all this activity is systematically avoided. In every case the action is aborted into formulaic and negating phrases. The SAS will be taking a 'hard long look at the ground', they'll be 'liaising', 'watching', 'reporting', 'training', 'working', 'operating', 'gathering intelligence', 'hiding up', 'surviving', and finally – 'acting'. At all times Snow is careful not to suggest that the SAS will actually *do* any of the terrible things on which their reputation is based; anything, in short, which would render their presence effective, even though that presence, we are reminded, has by itself 'struck fear into the heart of the enemy'. As Snow closes his piece with the words

that's why they, the SAS, believe that if anyone can find
the killers who strike by stealth, they can,

we are driven by the way the message itself is constructed
towards the response 'but they can't'. But successful or not,
it is enough for Snow to have made the SAS a culturally
identifiable unit.

This does not mean, of course, that the language of the
news is necessarily articulating uncritical enthusiasm for
established myths in order to create an artificial cultural
consensus. Even in Peter Snow's discourse there is enough
contradiction among the various responses triggered to
negate much of the confident tone of effective expertise, as
we have seen. In his effort to claw the potentially deviant
SAS back into socio-centrality, Snow has to deflect adverse
responses. The currently unwelcome associations of their
undercover role are such that he has to work hard: 'They've
been, *not entirely of their own choosing*, the undercover men.'
They are available to 'shoot it out' – but only '*if necessary*' –
with IRA gunmen. And their relationship with the ordinary
soldier, who is far more socio-central as one of 'our lads',
needs very careful handling:

> That is why the government is *making it clear tonight* that
> the Special Air Service will *not* be doing *anything very much
> out of the ordinary*, but *just* doing it *perhaps* a *bit* better,
> *because of their training*, than the *average* soldier is *able* to.

Here two positive myths about the army – the 'com-
mando' and the 'our-lads' myths – collide with such force
that the discourse seems to lose all momentum. It *cannot*
disguise the contradictions it has raised.

The Irish themselves need no such careful handling.
While Snow is clawing the SAS into the centre, he is by a
tacit converse action pushing the Irish as the actual or
potential enemy in the opposite direction. Here the method
is negative, unstated, but later in the bulletin it emerges as
a positively articulated attempt to signify the Irish as cultur-

ally deviant. We shall examine how it is done in chapter 8. For now it is sufficient to notice the paradoxical effect of Snow's successful attempt to bring the SAS into line with other culturally validated myths about the army. The British army's cultural function now is not to invade, conquer, win wars or even to be in the killing business at all. Its cultural function for the last generation has been to withdraw from Britain's shrinking hegemony; to set a brave, well-trained, technological face upon defeat. The SAS has been identified by Snow with central myths more usually applied to commandos, and its men have been identified as regular – if slightly better than average – army troops. Hence, according to the terms of the institutional third order of mythology, they must inevitably but paradoxically prove ineffective. And the mythology becomes self-fulfilling as Snow associates the SAS with known army myths at the expense of effectiveness. Having watched this bulletin, members of our culture were no doubt prepared for the subsequent inability of the SAS to change the situation in Northern Ireland.

Interestingly, the second main news story also has a militaristic slant. It concerns the Anglo-Icelandic fishing dispute known as the Cod War. Once again the individual is celebrated, this time in the shape of Captain Robert Gerken of the navy frigate *Andromeda*. His vessel has been in collision with the Icelandic coastguard vessel *Thor*, and he radios his own account to ITN. We can perhaps 'translate' the captain's report as it comes in:[1]

> . . . my assessment was that we were
> – *expert judgement*
> gonna have a collision
> – *but cool-headed (deadpan)*

[1] We have transcribed all statements verbatim, since some apparently ungrammatical usage substantially modifies the meanings of messages. But without showing the corresponding visual images this transcription may appear to show unrehearsed interviewees, especially, at a disadvantage.

and therefore at that stage
— *decision-maker*
I ordered
— *leader*
emergency full ahead
— *crisis language (war-film myths)*
and put port, er, rudder, full port rudder
— *but precise*
to try and swing my stern away from her stem as it
was coming er into my, towards my stern . . .
— *personal responsibility for 'my' ship, but no emotion towards the
enemy — 'it'.*

Note how neatly 'it' is identified as the aggressor, despite the
apparently analytical style of reporting. But once again this
individual mythology is contradicted by the institutional
mythology, which knows that Britain is eventually going to
lose the Cod War. Again, history proved this bulletin absolutely right: Britain did indeed lose. The knowledge of
ultimate defeat is inherent in the subsequent interview with
a naval 'expert', Captain John Cox, who is asked to 'explain'
the rammings. He does so by 'showing' with authoritative-
looking if somewhat mystifying diagrams, as well as
explanations, that the various collisions are not caused by
politics, or history, or Icelanders, but by fate:

Now *should* er der, an Icelandic gunboat try, as is common
practice, to get round the stern of a frigate to get at a
trawler, *it'll find itself* coming into the suction area, and as
it comes in and tries to slow down to get round the stern,
you can see what's happened; it *loses* all manoeuvrability *and
at that stage collision is absolutely inevitable . . . Today's I don't
understand, and nor does Captain Gerken.* It *appeared* that they
were both ships were on a steady course . . . and *then
suddenly* er the gunboat *Thor* turned towards, and *had it not
been for Captain Gerken* going full ahead and altering his
wheel hard a-port it *would have*, the *Thor would have* hit the
Andromeda er even further er forward, if I can put it that

way, in an unprotected place, and *would may've* gone straight through the engine room and straight through the dining room *like a knife through butter*.

The second order myths of technological skill on the part of the British captain, and of individual adventure at sea are highly visible at the surface, but they are negated by the third order of mythology, which makes them reactive to an arbitrary fate – in the convincing guise of Icelandic skippers who do not have the British reluctance to initiate action. Captain Cox's catalogue of possible disasters in the conditional tense serves at once to demonstrate the skill of the captain in avoiding them, and the inability of the institution he represents – be that the navy or the government – actually to admit to carrying out the violence that an armed frigate intrinsically represents. However, determination to act is not the missing ingredient here. What prevents aggressiveness on the part of the frigate in this bulletin is our culture. The newsreader has to assure us at the outset that

no one aboard either ship was hurt.

When the collisions are described, we are told that a 'small' hole was 'put' in the Icelandic ship. It does seem that in reality British aggression is possible, but there appears to be a kind of cultural embargo on reports about it. ITN had a reporter, Norman Rees, on board the Icelandic gunboat at the centre of this encounter, and he is able to give an eye-witness report of the manoeuvres:

At one stage the *Andromeda* had sailed within feet of *us*, her warning sirens blaring . . . *I saw* the *Andromeda* approaching *us* at high speed from the stern of the gunboat. It overtook *us* with both vessels on a converging course.

But he is *unable* to 'see' the actual collision:

According to Thor's skipper . . . *he* dropped his engine speed and tried to turn away to avoid a collision. But *he claims* that the frigate herself turned at the last moment so that

Andromeda's stern *would* side-swipe the gunboat's bow. The *Thor*'s deck shook under the force of the collision . . .

Rees's eyewitness language changes abruptly into reporter language, even though he must have been able to observe the changes in direction of each ship just as well as the skipper. He avoids having to say 'she hit us' or 'we hit her' by the apparently dramatic 'the *Thor*'s deck shook', but that phrase, describing the effect of the collision and not the collision itself, also paradoxically serves to mask intentional aggression on the part of the British frigate. Rees's apparent blindness is culturally determined, however, since his report articulates perfectly the journalistic codes of impartiality, even at the expense of his own observation. Even so, his report might still be suspect, because of his position among the (deviant) Icelanders, so the newsreader 'balances' it by announcing that the frigate's captain will 'describe *exactly* what happened'.

The contradictory mythologies of individuals versus institutions develops throughout the bulletin. There follows a series of home affairs stories; the government is presented as ineffectual because of its inability to 'get its figures right' in both a story about the junior doctors' dispute with the Department of Health and a story about cut-backs in mortgages granted by local government. In the first story, the individual alibi is provided by the doctors' leader on the one hand, who presents himself as a fair and patient man faced with insuperable idiocy, and by ITN's own home affairs correspondent on the other hand, who presents himself in an investigatory role – teasing out government figures from a deliberately confused tangle. This theme of bungling statistics is clearly imposed on the material by the ITN scriptwriters: it is perceived as newsworthy to the extent that it shows government inefficiency.

The advertisements sandwiched into the bulletin play a major and positive role in asserting the primacy of individual relationships and action, and it is significant that they foreground women, as the focal point of families, and as the practical copers-with-life. The first advertisement responds to the institutional problems of the economy (which have just been featured) with an appeal to self-help – a needle-craft manual which enables the buyer to save money by her own action. This is the individual antidote to the third-order failure (despite second-order appearances) of our cultural endeavours out-there.

This pattern is reiterated throughout the second half of the news which concentrates on the bungling this time of foreign governments. At the very end, the tailpiece (which in this case does indeed wag the dog), inverts the customary emphasis and celebrates directly and without an obvious institutional peg an individual success story:

> Here at home a man who a few years ago had no job and what he calls no prospects has been named shepherd of the year . . . He's Bill Graham who's thirty-nine and he lost his arm after a motor-cycle accident in his twenties. Now he looks after more than 1000 sheep . . . He went to see his present employer without much hope of getting the job of assistant shepherd. But he did get it and now he's chief shepherd but he's refused to take a pay rise. He takes part in regular competitions an' he's well-known around the country . . .

The man is filmed with his sheepdog, to whom he gives priority over the interviewer. Rather than answer a question put directly to him he whistles up the dog. His reality takes precedence over that of the (institutional) interviewer. He embodies many of the second-order signs of the news as a whole. His economic position, like the culture's, was bleak. But by individual perseverance, even when both his luck and his natural attributes were truncated, he secured the means to survive, and went on to newsworthy success. He is fully involved in his society despite his lonely task – he competes and is well-known and respected for his skills. He is an iconic representation of the 'truth' of the mythology of the individual, and of its ultimate primacy over the mythology of the institution; a specific man who is at the same time a metonymic representative of his culture's values and a metaphor for individual success. In Bill Graham, all three orders of signification are presented simultaneously. He is a walking mythology.

It is no accident that after this tailpiece the same headlines that were read out in a grim-faced, serious manner at the opening of the bulletin can now be repeated – almost verbatim – in a cheerful, smiling tone. Bill Graham has single-handedly set the world to rights.

7 AUDIENCES

I F television can speak meaningfully to vast cross-cultural audiences, how can it at the same time take account of divisions within particular societies? In order to be able to understand the nature of the relationship between the television medium and the constituent groups of its culture, we should first indicate briefly what the divisions within society are to which it *can* respond. In a recent study of the contours of class relations in a society such as ours, Westergaard and Resler (1976) have attempted to show how the social divisions with which we are all familiar by simple observation are actually structured.

For this purpose they have revived a distinction first proposed by Marx (e.g. 1968, pp. 117f. and 170–1) between class *in itself* and class *for itself*. Many of the implications of this idea go beyond the scope of our study, but there is an important distinction to be made. Class *in itself* involves the *objective existence* of classes produced by a social structure deriving ultimately from what Marx variously terms the material, social or economic 'conditions of existence'. These classes are differentiated from one another by inequalities of power, wealth, security, opportunity and position, and the crucial source of inequality, say Westergaard and Resler, is private ownership and the associated control of the productive apparatus. Class *in itself*, deriving from in-equalities based on economic 'conditions of existence', exists irrespective of how people themselves (whether they be victims or beneficiaries of inequality) see and respond to their class condition.

But people's response to their objective class situation does give rise to the secondary notion of class *for itself*. This is the (sometimes only potential) awareness among people of a *common identity* springing from their common experience. The response can take different forms: common identity can be voiced as a sense of common interests to be pursued in opposition to other classes in society, as for instance in the Labour movement or the trade unions; or it can be seen more in competitive terms than in solidarity. That is, people's response to their objective class condition can produce a widespread predominance of what Westergaard and Resler call 'individual anxieties about personal *social* status without *political* impetus' (1976, p. 3); in short, keeping up with the Joneses.

It is important for us to have made this distinction be-cause we suggest that in the world of television divisions between classes *in themselves* are rarely if ever presented as such. Television articulates the responses of people to their class condition, not the class condition itself. Hence it is primarily a medium for the expression of classes *for them-selves*. Here again, however, the expression is rarely one of oppositional solidarity of either the dominant or the sub-ordinate class towards one another. Rather, television – along with most other commercial enterprises – exploits the competitive fragmentation among people who belong to what is objectively the same, subordinate, class. Hence social divisions on television as elsewhere emerge as a kind of sliding scale of social stratification as opposed to primary class division.

Nevertheless it is necessary to remember that despite social stratification, and the consequent differentials of status between, say, professionals and managers on the one hand and blue-collar and manual workers on the other, all these groups are objectively members of the same class *in itself*. Managers and professionals may be relatively privileged in the premium they are able to set on their labour power, and they may be relatively more committed to the existing structure of social relationships. But it remains the case that many of them are ultimately just as dependent on selling their labour power as blue-collar workers. Their lack of control over property, and hence the conditions of their own employment and production, results in an actual or potential insecurity which provides a basis for 'identity of interest'. This is television's starting-point: its 'mass mode' is merely a recognition of the basically similar 'social conditions of existence' that obtain among apparently widely disparate groups.

Audience responses

Just as the economic and social system of capitalism has grown and transformed itself over a long period, so have the responses of people to it. There is indeed a sense in which the differences in class and status that we can observe at any one time should more properly be thought of as a constant flux than as a fixed hierarchy of relations. Social mobility, changed historical conditions and changes in what Marx (1968, p. 117) calls the 'entire superstructure of distinct and peculiarly formed sentiments, illusions, modes of thought and views of life' have produced among all groups in our culture a complex set of interrelations with other groups, a pervasive intersubjectivity whereby clear-cut distinctions between them are difficult to discern. The same applies to individuals – each one of us holds mutually contradictory beliefs about our position in society, and we respond to our condition in different ways at the same time.

Parkin (1972, pp. 79–102) has shown how these responses can be categorized into what he terms 'meaning systems', of which three are distinguishable. They are:

1 *The dominant system.* This presents what might be called the 'official' version of class relations. It promotes endorsement of the existing inequality, and leads to a response among members of the subordinate class that can be described either as *deferential*, or as *aspirational*. That is, a 'dominant' definition of the situation leads people to accept the existing distribution of jobs, power, wealth, etc. Either they simply defer to 'the way things are', or they aspire to an individual share of the available rewards.

2 *The subordinate system.* This defines a moral framework which, while prepared to endorse the dominant system's claims to overall control of the economic processes, nevertheless reserves the right to negotiate a better share for particular groups at any time. It promotes *accommodative* or *negotiated* responses to inequality, and can be seen at work for instance in the attitudes behind the notion of 'them' and 'us', and in the collective bargaining of trade-unionism, whereby the *framework* of the reward structure is accepted. All that is at issue is the share to be had by various communities or groups.

3 *The radical system.* The source for this is the mass political party based on that section of the subordinate class whose identity of interest is expressed in working-class solidarity. It is class-conscious (unlike the previous two meaning systems) in that it rejects the frameworks by which one class achieves a dominant position, and so it promotes an *oppositional* response to inequality.

Parkin comments that in most western societies all three meaning systems tend to influence the social and political perceptions of most people in the subordinate class. Hall (1973) discusses the implications of Parkin's three systems in the context of the television message. He suggests that the dominant, negotiated and oppositional responses form the basis for the codes which are used by both the addresser and the addressee of the television message; that is, by both the encoder and the decoder. The latent meaning of programmes is usually encoded in the dominant code. Hence a preferred meaning emerges at the connotative level. But the 'bits' of information emanating from the screen will, no matter how they are encoded, be given a syntagmatic structure by the viewer, who also uses one of the three codes to decode the message. Since the code used is derived from the viewer's general social experience as well as from his response to the particular message, we find that the second-order meanings of the television message engage at the moment of decoding with the various meaning systems of the audience members. It is at this moment that the final meaning of any television message is negotiated.

Since the three codes (and their various sub-categories) are available to all viewers at the moment of meaning, then the same message can be decoded according to different codes, corresponding to the social experience of the decoder, and yet remain meaningful for all groups. Furthermore, this characteristic is one of the most important safeguards that the viewer has against direct influence from television. To take a clear-cut example, if a story about an industrial dispute is presented in a news or current affairs programme, and its latent or connotative meaning suggests that the dispute is bad for business, then it has probably been encoded according to the dominant code. If the viewer has an interest in the outcome of the dispute, he might well accept the dominant argument of the 'need to restrain wages' in the 'national interest', but still make an exception in the particular case. In other words, using the negotiated code the viewer's deference on matters of 'grand signification' bears little or no relation to his willingness to demand improvements in his own particular lot. (For the television treatment of industrial disputes see the Glasgow Media Group's study, *Bad News*, 1976.)

Life-style and class condition

However, there are many symbolic or cultural distinctions which each sector of the subordinate class uses to set what is usually called its 'life-style' apart from that of other sectors. The manifest content of television both draws upon and blurs these symbolic distinctions. Various life-styles are presented with clear signals that they derive from one status group and not another. However, the very fact that they are presented to a mass audience translates such class-based programmes as *The Wheel-Tappers' and Shunters' Social Club*, *Till Death Us Do Part*, *Coronation Street*, etc. out of working-class culture and into popular culture. Popular culture appeals to a far wider audience than the traditional working class. Nevertheless, that wider audience is still drawn from what we have called the subordinate class *in itself*.

Despite the fact that popular culture and working-class culture are not the same thing, certain sociologists have commented on the 'rising affluence' of the traditional working class, and on the 'middle-class' values discerned in popular entertainment such as film or television. Combining these data, they have suggested that television performs a function of 'anticipatory socialization', whereby people use the mediated view of status groups higher than their own (which they see on television) as models they can emulate. The idea is that people can then learn the characteristic language, behaviour, and habits of the aspired-to status group in order to gain entry and then adjust to that group.

This thesis has been elaborated by Mendelsohn (1966) and can be seen as a variation of the *embourgeoisement* thesis, which on the evidence of apparently widespread affluence in the 1960s sought to show that old class divisions were breaking down as members of the working class 'joined' the middle class in increasing numbers. However, this ill-named thesis mistook the clothes for the man; it took life-style to be the same thing as material conditions of existence. One of its chief failings in the present context is that although mass entertainment in a period of full employment does indeed provide most people with leisure pursuits formerly reserved for their betters, it does not by that token seduce them into a different class. Pursuit of what Mendelsohn calls the good life on the part of the subordinate class does not, in other words, magically transform it into the dominant class; even when the model used to define the good life is supplied to the have-nots by the haves. In fact, as Piepe *et al.* (1975, p. 165) conclude in their study of television and the working class, the 'commitment' of workers who have apparently undergone *embourgeoisement* is 'at bottom a pragmatic one': acceptance of dominant definitions of the situation is contingent upon the dominant order, literally, coming up with the goods.

On this basis we can perhaps begin to discern the nature of the relationship between the television medium and the divisions in a society like ours. The *mass* medium is paradoxically classless – in the sense that most of its content derives from the experience of and is directed towards the members of what we can now see is the class to which the vast majority of us belong: the subordinate class *in itself*.

It is noteworthy that there are very few television representations of the dominant class; that is, the owners of the productive apparatus. On British television there has been a successful series based on the directors of a large company, *The Brothers*. But it is significant that much of the interest in the plot revolves around the original *family* of owners, the Hammonds, being subjected to the pressures of truly capitalist power. This power is represented by the character the viewers love to hate, banker Paul Merroney. He has married into a family of vast inherited wealth and influence. Merroney's ambitious, cold personal manner, and willingness to discard traditional practices serves to contrast the like usness of the Hammond family. Over a period of several years, viewers have watched him, after joining the board as a condition for a loan – to 'safeguard the bank's interest' – transform a medium-sized independent family company into an impersonal appendage of a capitalist empire. The real capitalist power behind Merroney is rarely given substance, though in one crucial episode Merroney is seen persuading his father-in-law in intimate club-like surroundings to part with several hundred thousand pounds to back his schemes – the kind of power with which neither the fictive Hammonds nor the real audience can compete.

In other words, *The Brothers*, even while it is a series which at the denotative or manifest level is about the property-owning class, succeeds *as television* precisely where it transforms that class, in the shape of the Hammond family, into a part of the subordinate class. The life-style can be as glamorous and dominant as you like, but the class condition at the connotative level usually emerges as like-us: subordinate. In fact, the glamour of *The Brothers'* conspicuous consumption has a metonymic relationship with our own life-styles as viewers – we share the culture that values this life-style, and we may even possess some of the objects and attributes that such a series celebrates. We are drawn into this well-heeled milieu, and not debarred from it by virtue of our lack of wealth.

8 THE MODES OF TELEVISION

IN most discussions of television the audience is characterized in one of two ways: either as the individual
viewer, or as the many millions of viewers for any one
programme. But the audience normally experiences *itself* in
neither of these ways. Of course each viewer is aware both
of his individuality and of his membership of a large group.
But while actually watching, most people are part of a
family audience.

This has important consequences for the way television
relates to its society, and for the way the audience responds
to it. Mendelsohn (1966) has shown, with regard to mass
entertainment in general, that

> people who seek and experience mass entertainment do
> not do so as isolated, autonomous individuals – as theor-
> ists of 'mass society' suggest – but, rather as group
> members, and in social contexts that call for a high degree
> of interpersonal communication. (p. 74)

If this is true of the experience of going out to the cinema,
then clearly it is even more true of staying at home with the
TV (see McQuail 1975, pp. 186–93). Indeed, the family
context of television watching is a crucial part of its meaning
as Hawkes (1973) has argued:

... an 'evening', say, spent watching television will have a quality of multifariousness within a much larger and more significant unity; that of the home, the known surroundings, the family or other 'setting' in which the response to television usually takes place. An isolated picture-frame 'cynosure' does not monopolize the attention, because the screen itself sheds light on, and draws *to* itself a known and literally 'inhabited' environment. Such an environment encourages audience participation, reinforced by the fact that the members of the audience usually constitute a group who know each other intimately. (p. 233)

And we should remember that, as Frank Parkin (1972, pp. 14–15) has pointed out, the 'appropriate social unit of the class system' is not the individual, it is the family. In other words television slots neatly into the actual social structure established among its audience.

Just as we should not be taken in by the implications of the term 'mass audience', so we should avoid the mistake of regarding the 'mass medium' of television as undifferentiated for all users. Stephenson (1967) argues that the concept of 'massness' should be treated with caution even when applied to the movement of industrial products:

Mass marketing of mass-produced products in free economies has tended to hide the fact that the products become idiosyncratic by the time they reach a buyer; it is difficult to find two cars exactly alike because differences of colour, interiors, accessories, engines, and so on make it possible for everyone to have a car for himself, different in some way from almost any other. (p. 35)

We have seen how the television message itself is made idiosyncratic by the time it is decoded by its viewers – each family audience will negotiate its own stance towards the message and so modify its meaning. Stephenson applies the term of 'convergent selectivity' to the phenomenon of large numbers of individuals or groups who freely choose similar opportunities for themselves; his extreme example of convergent selectivity is the gold rush. In relation to television he suggests that the phenomenon produces a bond between the viewers and the medium that is the more powerful because it is freely entered into:

> It is fair to say, also, that in the immediate experience of convergent selectivity there is a heightened self-awareness, a greater receptivity in the person. One is a free man in front of a television set, or with a newspaper in one's hands, to a degree not achieved before by man in his long history. (*ibid.*)

The 'mass' audience is relatively free from direct media-originated constraint. It is in a literally 'familiar' environment, and each viewer or family group is able to respond to the television message in terms that are intimately meaningful for themselves personally.

But even this context for the medium would not guarantee its communicative success unless the modes of presentation employed also responded to the actuality of the viewers' own situation. As we have argued, such viewers do not necessarily share the *same* situation. Our case for the resolution of this apparent paradox is an essentially simple one. Television responds to the divisions within society in much the same way as society itself accommodates those divisions for most practical purposes. We are not arguing here for a uniform and stifling – not to say mythical – consensus, operating within a plural society. On the contrary, we accept the view of Westergaard and Resler (1976) when they argue that

> Contrary to the assumptions characteristic of 'functionalist' theorizing, complex societies are not usually harmonious, blandly consensual, in stable equilibrium or for ever on their way to it. It is far closer to the truth, if still too crude and sweeping a generalization, to see them as

perennially on the verge of instability. The cleavages inside them are there all the time, as potential triggers of
change, even of collapse. Yet divided though they are,
they rarely plunge over the edge. That paradox – the
common co-existence of cleavage and continuity – is at
its most acute, however, in the case of capitalist societies.
(p. 7)

Television is itself a major agency for the daily enactment
of that 'common co-existence of cleavage and continuity'.
Its modes of presentation are derived from both dominant
and subordinate codes, and the tension between different
sectors of society is actually *enacted* – not so much in the
denotative content of the messages as in the *way* those messages are presented.

Oral logic

How then are the contradictions which we find in society at
large presented in the television medium? To begin an
answer to this question it might be useful once again to
return to our January 1976 *News at Ten* bulletin (see chapter
6). This bulletin displays a characteristic common to all
television discourse which we have termed 'oral logic'. The
full implications of this term will emerge as we pursue our
argument, but in simple terms, it suggests that television's
meanings are arrived at through the devices of spoken discourse fused with visual images, rather than through the
structures of formal logic. This means that apparent in-
consistencies or lapses in logic are not necessarily faults in
television discourse. They must be seen as aspects of a different kind of logic: as part of a process whose aim is to produce
fully satisfactory and plausible meaning; a process which
offers us myths with which we are already familiar, and
seeks to convince us that these myths are appropriate to
their context.

We described in chapter 6 how in our *News at Ten* the

ITN defence correspondent, Peter Snow, used his own kind of oral logic to claw back into a culturally central position the potentially deviant SAS troops. By the same token he implies (while never actually stating) that the Irish people *are* deviant. The more he centralizes the SAS, the less like-us the Irish appear, since they supply the enemy for the SAS. Snow articulates this process mainly in terms of the SAS. He is followed, however, by Gerald Seymour who takes a positive role in the converse process of creating a deviant identity for the Irish. He reports on the search for the perpe-trators of the Bessbrook Massacre of two days previously, when ten Protestants were killed. (It was this massacre which provided the immediate stimulus for the govern-ment's announcement to send in the SAS.) Far from articu-lating all the contradictory notions we may hold about Northern Ireland, Seymour seems to ignore them alto-gether:

> The new troops and police who have been sent to South Armagh to track down the gang who shot dead ten pro-testants on Monday night have been issued with this photograph of B— S—, born in Bessbrook where the murdered men came from and now living south of the border in County Louth. S—, aged thirty-one, and dark haired, has long been wanted for questioning by detec-tives in Northern Ireland investigating what they classify as serious terrorist crimes in the area. S— has never been in custody in the North, but he appeared three years ago in the Dublin Special Criminal Court on arms charges, and spent two years in prison after conviction. He ap-pealed against the sentence, thereby breaking IRA con-ventions in recognizing the court, and was reported to have been thrown out of the movement. But shortly after his release he was back again on the wanted list compiled by military intelligence operating in South Armagh.

Seymour's argument continues in this vein, but even in this extract we can see how he removes us from the complexities of Irish politics into another world – that of the simple individualist causation of police courts. This is reinforced by the visual code: a traditional 'mugshot' of S—, which is held on screen for so long (41 seconds) that the contradictions which previous items in the Northern Ireland sequence might have exposed are virtually suffocated. The screen at this point holds very little information: the photograph is black and white, a still, and of such a shape that it fails to fill the screen. Hence most of our attention is diverted to the words. Seymour performs his bardic role here by translating a social, institutional and inchoate *reality* into a familiar individualist *mythology*.

Of course Seymour selects the myth structure of individual criminal deviance from a paradigm of possible choices which is neither arbitrary nor unlimited. Other possible signifiers for S— and the police/army could include, for instance, those of 'freedom fighters' and 'occupying forces'. Clearly to choose these at the moment would be culturally deviant or *eccentric*, and Seymour's bardic function precludes such choices. Further, the events (the signifieds) themselves constrain his choice – the mythology must be a plausible translation of the reality. In addition, Seymour's sociocentrality presupposes that his choice will be governed to a large extent by the preferred meanings of what we have earlier called the dominant meaning system in our culture.

Having selected this mythology, Seymour fits reality to it. The oral logic seems to run as follows: the recent events in Northern Ireland are merely criminal; hence they are a matter not for the army but for detectives and the police who are mentioned nowhere else in the Northern Ireland sequence. If there's a crime, runs the logic, there must be a criminal. This man is clearly the individual in question. And he is the individual in question because of the semiotic context within which his name appears. Seymour does not indicate any evidence that connects him with the Bessbrook Massacre, beyond his local associations and his previous court appearance. That court appearance is of course very important. It can convince us that we are not party to the witch-hunting of an innocent man. Furthermore Seymour implies that the man is connected with the IRA at the very moment when his evidence (S—'s violation of IRA codes) suggests that S— had no link with that organization. S— is condemned not by what he has really done, but by the police-court images, which are powerfully familiar both in news and fiction. The intractable political problems of Northern Ireland are thus subsumed into a familiar and readily available mythology – that of the criminal and his institutional counterpart, the court of justice. That myth-ology has the added advantage in this context that it can confidently articulate our relationship with people who are culturally peripheral by definition, and people who are, moreover, single and anonymous individuals who neverthe-less act out their parts in public.

The confidence inherent in this mythology is important for Seymour's effect. He articulates positively a way of seeing whereby the Irish are no longer like-us, and for whom S—, merely by being presented on television, be-comes a metonym. Seymour's story presents us with a myth-ology which bears a metaphoric, equivalent relationship to the events he describes, enabling him to gather together the data he selects from the reality out-there and make it into a coherent syntagm.

Through the mechanism of this equivalent way of seeing we are enabled not merely to understand the events, but we are also offered an orientation towards them – a way of judging them. As a result, Seymour is able to offer us the evidence for a change in our attitudes towards the Irish – they are deviant – and in addition the preferred direction in which that change should occur – their deviancy is criminal and can be dealt with as such. However, we should re-member that Seymour is only offering us this way of seeing – it is not in his power to enforce its acceptance. As we have noted, the individual viewer, usually under the powerful influence of his or her domestic environment, negotiates a response to the proffered message, testing it against his or her total cultural experience.

Seymour's story certainly passes one part of this test – it can be understood easily. Whether or not it is accepted as an appropriate way of understanding the complexities of Northern Ireland politics is another matter, which will be decided by a much larger and more diffuse cultural process, a kind of collective bargaining whereby dominant definitions of the situation are negotiated and established. This process includes the mass audience's response to messages such as these, while the messages themselves constitute a valuable indication of the state of that collective bargaining at any one time. Hence neither Snow nor Seymour present us with finished meanings; both offer possible interpretations of events out-there which may or may not become accepted as the appropriate way of seeing that particular reality. In short, if the metaphor fits, we'll wear it.

Oral and literate traditions in television discourse

One of the implications of the preceding argument is that despite the feedback from people who watch, the collective bargaining seems to operate with convenient advantages for the dominant section of society, whose preferred or sociocentral interpretations are most likely to be represented in the television message, and whose spokesman our bardic newsman might appear to be. However, television is not a simple medium, and its meanings are not communicated simply. While it is true that many messages, and particularly the verbal content of news messages, are encoded according to the dominant definition of the situation, we shall try to show that this does not oblige us to conclude tautologically that 'those who are dominant must dominate'. True as this is, it is not the end of the matter. We shall devote the rest of this chapter to an account of the way in which the medium responds to and even embodies a contradictory set of ways of seeing.

Take once again our notion of an 'oral logic'. How does it differ from what we normally think of as logic? The answer is to be found in the origin of logic, which, as Goody and Watt (1962) point out in their seminal study of the consequences of alphabetic literacy, stems from the invention of literate discourse in classical Greece: 'It is surely significant that it was only in the days of the first widespread alphabetic culture that the idea of "logic" – of an immutable and impersonal mode of discourse – appears to have arisen' (p. 331). However, television discourse is not 'immutable and impersonal' in nature, and its mode is the reverse of literate or formal logic: its mode is that of rhetoric. For instance, the television message is validated by its context, by the opposition of elements (often visual/verbal), and not by the deductive requirements of the syllogism. The kind of consistency which requires an alphabetic means of recording and retrieval in order to be known, and which imposes its own kinds of constraints on, for instance, the style of the novel, is alien to the television discourse.

But the official culture of our society has, until the advent of television, been conducted through pervasively literate modes. Ever since the Elizabethan period when print-literacy first became an essential attribute of men of the world, there has been what can be thought of as a 'cultural lag' between those men and women who in Laslett's (1971) words 'could only think, and talk, and sing and play, and till the soil, and tend the beasts, and make things, like barrels and ploughs and windmills . . .'; and those men who could, in addition to these things, 'also read and write, and record, and refer again, and criticize, and tell others what was the truth of the matter and what should be done about it' (p. 207).

There is evidence to suggest these distinctions still exist in our own day. Bernstein (1973) for instance has formulated a theory which suggests that the speech of working-class and that of middle-class speakers tends to be organized according to different 'codes', which he calls 'restricted' codes and 'elaborated' codes respectively. His work has drawn a great deal of criticism, largely based on a feeling that his names for the two codes imply a negative evaluation of working-class speech.

Bernstein has argued that in the process of socializing a child there are differently based codes for different groups: for the basis of the *restricted* code is in 'communalized roles, realizing context-dependent meanings, i.e. particularistic meaning orders', while the basis of the *elaborated* code is in 'individualized roles realizing context-independent universalistic meanings' (p. 205). The codes are so called because in the elaborated version the speaker selects from a 'relatively extensive range of alternatives', and in the restricted version the number of these alternatives is, according to Bernstein, 'severely limited' – hence for this code it is much easier to predict the pattern of the organizing elements.

A pure form of the restricted code would be 'ritualistic modes of communication': hence 'individual intent can be signalled only through the non-verbal components of the situation, i.e. intonation, stress, expressive features, etc. Specific verbal planning will be minimal'. The social forms which produce the restricted code are of the kind where there is 'some common set of closely shared identifications self-consciously held by the members, where immediacy of the relationship is stressed'. Its background is therefore 'communal'. How things are said is more important than what is said, and the content of this speech is likely to be 'concrete, descriptive and narrative rather than analytical or abstract'. The major function of the restricted code is to 'reinforce the *form* of the social relationship (a warm and inclusive relationship) by restricting the verbal signalling of individuated responses'. Where there are channels for an individuated response, as in humour, wit, or a joking relationship, the effect of the individuated response is to reinforce the solidarity of the social relationship.

The elaborated code, on the other hand, 'becomes the vehicle for individual responses'. A major purpose of this code is the preparation and delivery of 'relatively *explicit* meaning'. It promotes a high level of structural organization and word selection. The code promotes a tendency towards abstraction (pp. 93–5).

We can see that the language used by Bernstein is rich in allusions to the kind of relationship we have been proposing between television and its audience: in Bernstein's terms television uses the restricted code. However, Bernstein himself is aware of the dangers of discussing class differences in these terms:

> One of the difficulties of this approach is to avoid implicit value judgements about the relative worth of speech systems and the cultures which they symbolize. Let it be said immediately that a restricted code gives access to a vast potential of meanings, of delicacy, subtlety and diversity of cultural forms, to a unique aesthetic the basis of which in condensed symbols may influence the form of the imagining. Yet, in complex industrialized societies its differently-focused experience may be disvalued and humiliated within schools, or seem, at best, to be irrelevant to the educational endeavour. For the schools are predicated upon elaborated code and its system of social relationships. Although an elaborated code does not entail any specific value system, the value system of the middle class penetrates the texture of the very learning context itself. (p. 211)

In short, the restricted code is only restricted to the extent that it falls short of the requirements of the literate, individualist dominant orders of meaning. Moreover, as Parkin (1972) has pointed out,

> ... the characteristic speech patterns and linguistic usages of the dominant class are generally regarded as 'correct', or what counts as the grammar of the language; the usages of the subordinate class are often said to be 'incorrect' or ungrammatical where they differ from the former. (p. 83)

This remains the case even when sociologists and linguists have pointed out the lack of any factual foundation for such a stance. For instance the American linguist, Labov, has in a brilliant study shown that the speech of working-class Negro English speakers in New York is 'disvalued' not for any intrinsic failing but because of class-based preferences for certain structures of speech. Comparing the speech of two Negroes, Labov comments:

> The initial impression of Charles M as a good speaker is simply our long-conditioned reaction to middle-class verbosity: we know that people who use these devices are educated people, and we are inclined to credit them with saying something intelligent. Our reactions are accurate in one sense: Charles M is more educated than Larry. But is he more rational, more logical or more intelligent? Is he any better at thinking out a problem to its solution? Does he deal more easily with abstractions? There is no reason to think so. Charles M succeeds in letting us know that he is educated, but in the end we do not know what he is trying to say, and neither does he. (1969, p. 200)

Non-standard English, then, is certainly logical in its structure, but its non-literate logic is of a kind which is commonly disvalued because it does not conform to the expected norms of literate logic. Of course it is not merely a matter of logic – there is a tendency for many of the multifarious and often localized forms, dialects and codes of working-class speech to be disvalued, whether they succeed as effective communication in their context or not. Hence it is perhaps not surprising that a medium which derives its modes of presentation from such speech should be disvalued in some quarters for that reason alone.

But there is a further reason for the hostility with which television is greeted by certain critics. It concerns the medium's fundamental non-literacy; or rather, the apparently cavalier habit it seems to foster of 'reducing' to non-literate form any matter it deals with. In fact there is a tension embodied in the television message that we can trace back to the differences in the esteem which our culture traditionally accords to oral and literate discourse respectively. Bernstein's elaborated code tends to be the preferred mode of discourse for the literate controllers and encoders of television messages. But, as we have suggested, it is not easily employed in the encoding of television messages, precisely because it derives from literate discourse and shares many of its characteristics, i.e. a tendency to abstraction, universalization, and the effort after so-called explicit or consistent meaning.

In addition, Goody and Watt (1962) show how a literate society produces a social stratification based upon what people have read (p. 341). Literate culture, unlike oral culture, is very easy to avoid – you simply don't read the book. Its effects can be shallow or even, during schooling, negated by the 'very different and indeed often directly contradictory private oral traditions of the pupil's family and peer group'. The immediately available cultural repertoire of a literate society is so vast that any selection which an individual makes to produce a coherent view of life must in the end be a personal one, creating varieties of cultural patterns within the one society, which separate individual from individual.

We can say that the 'cultural lag' we have described, between, on the one hand, those people in a literate society who use the written word as an autonomous means of communication habitually in their everyday lives on the one hand, and, on the other, those people who while they are *able* to read and write tend not to for normal self-defining purposes, is perceived in modern society to be a cultural lag between the dominant and the subordinate classes respectively. In consequence, we can suggest that to the extent that this is the case, class distinctions become more than economic or status distinctions: class consciousness for each class is of a different *kind*. Williams's (1958) famous distinction between the 'modes' of culture goes some way towards this idea: for him working-class culture comprises 'the basic collective idea', while bourgeois culture comprises the 'basic individualist idea' (p. 313. See also Thompson 1968, pp. 462f.).

If there exists a significant section of the population whose perceptual codes are at least partly of a continuing oral character, then we can revise McQuail's (1975) judgement that it is impossible to test the effect of the introduction of media like printing and television because 'there are not separate cultures in modern society, one based on the electronic media and the other on print' (p. 91). Certainly, different media cannot generate entirely separate cultures, for as McQuail observes, 'the different forms of media are very much interdependent; film and television rely very much on "literary" convention, while printed communications rely on a wide diffusion of iconic images as a frame of reference' (*ibid.*). However, what we do suggest is that there are substantial and identifiable differences in the modes of perception that people bring to bear on those media, and that those differences are to a large extent class based. Furthermore, television is the first and so far the only medium which has institutionalized the interdependence described by McQuail. In other words, in the television medium the oral modes of perception and the dominant literate modes are for the first time caused to interact in one medium on a mass, or even a global, scale.

Goody and Watt (1962) have indicated the effects of this development: the channels of mass communication, they say,

derive much of their effectiveness as agencies of social orientation from the fact that their media do not have the abstract and solitary quality of reading and writing, but on the contrary share some of the nature and impact of the direct personal interaction which obtains in oral cultures. It may even be that these new modes of communicating sight and sound without any limit of time or place will lead to a new kind of culture: less inward and

individualistic than literate culture, probably, and shar-
ing some of the relative homogeneity, though not the
mutuality, of oral society. (p. 347)

In other words, one effect of a medium which combines the
distinct cultures we have been discussing, might be to lead
to a restructuring in the modes of perception of reality for
the culture as a whole (even though the interaction between
the two cultures is primarily, at this stage, one of contradiction between the modes of perception of different classes).
The best known proponent of this view is McLuhan, who
suggests that the 'mutuality' which Goody and Watt fail to
discern in television culture is in fact a necessary consequence of it. He makes a distinction between 'hot' media
and 'cool' media:

> There is a basic principle that distinguishes a hot medium
> like radio from a cool one like the telephone, or a hot
> medium like the movie from a cool one like TV. A hot
> medium is one that extends one single sense in 'high defi-
> nition'. High definition is the state of being well filled
> with data. A photograph is, visually, 'high definition'. A
> cartoon is 'low definition', simply because very little
> visual information is provided. Telephone is a cool
> medium, or one of low definition, because the ear is given
> a meager amount of information. And speech is a cool
> medium of low definition, because so little is given and so
> much has to be filled in by the listener. On the other
> hand, hot media do not leave so much to be filled in or
> completed by the audience. Hot media are, therefore,
> low in participation, and cool media are high in participa-
> tion or completion by the audience. (1964, p. 31)

Thus television, a cool medium, gives its audience plenty
to do. This view accords with our suggestion earlier that the
television message is made meaningful only at the moment
when the semiotic codes interlock with the cultural awareness *supplied by the viewer*, whose own context will play a part

in shaping that cultural awareness. Similarly the character-istic shared by both the television message and the so-called restricted code of working-class speakers, whereby a wide range of signifiers is used to represent a very limited range of signifieds, can now be seen as one which requires the viewer or respondent to participate fully in supplying the con-textual, moral or other framework in whose terms the signified becomes meaningful. In short, television is a 'cool' medium because the viewer does most of the work: the screen supplies mere metonyms, we make them meaningful.

We have devoted a fair amount of space to this part of the argument because of its complexity and its unfamiliarity. However, it does not alter the *status* of the media languages, which is characterized at this stage in their development by the 'subordinate place they occupy in relation to a dominant culture which emphasizes linearity, rationality and verbal literacy' (McQuail 1975, p. 92). The implication of this historical matrix for the mode of television presentation is that, while television displays oral modes, the literate modes of the dominant class remain the dominant shaping force in the ideology of the programmers. For instance, literate modes were celebrated at length by Huw Wheldon, then managing director of BBC television, in his televised *Dimbleby Lecture*, where he claimed for British television that, 'in the first place', it 'rests on the *literary* and dramatic genius of the British people' (1976, p. 1).

We can set out in opposing columns the modes by which television is organized on the one hand, and the modes characteristic of dominant literate culture on the other. We call these modes oral and literate respectively.

Oral modes	Literate modes
dramatic	narrative
episodic	sequential
mosaic	linear
dynamic	static
active	artifact

concrete	abstract
ephemeral	permanent
social	individual
metaphorical	metonymic
rhetorical	logical
dialectical	univocal/'consistent'

However, since the television medium is fully incorporated into the processes of society as a whole, its final form results from the active tension between these modes.

Since most of the people who control television institutions are deeply committed to literate modes of perception, there is a systematic intervention on their part into its performances which exercises a limiting and transforming influence on its potential output. How that affects the messages as broadcast will be examined in the following chapters. At this point we can say that the process we have described has carried 'television culture' beyond the stage described by the anthropologist Claude Lévi-Strauss as one where

> we are no longer linked to our past by an oral tradition which implies direct contact with others (storytellers, priests, wise men, or elders), but by books amassed in libraries, books from which we endeavour – with extreme difficulty – to form a picture of their authors . . . The international organizations . . . have so far entirely failed to appreciate the loss of personal autonomy that has resulted from the expansion of the indirect forms of communication (books, photographs, press, radio, etc.). (1968, p. 366)

Television, according to our analysis of its message, function and mode, communicates a metonymic 'contact with others', in which all Lévi-Strauss's lost storytellers, priests, wise men or elders are restored to cultural visibility and to oral primacy: often indeed in the convincing guise of highly literate specialists, from newsreaders to scientific and artistic experts. This selective communication is what we have termed television's bardic function, and it restores much of the personal autonomy to the viewer in the sense that he supplies the conditions, both semiotic and social, under which any specific message becomes meaningful.

9 DANCE

I could have danced all night

I<small>T</small> is worth asking why dance figures so prominently in light entertainment on television, and what the relationship is between the dances we perform in discos and ballrooms, and programmes like *Come Dancing* and the staged spectacular dance on television. Uses and gratifications theory and functional theories say that light entertainment programmes satisfy our needs for diversion by reducing tension and offering us fantasy or escape. Semiotics asks the questions that come next – from what do they divert us, towards what, and how do they manage it?

Rust (1969) writes: 'One of the functions which dancing most clearly fulfils is that of "tension management" ' (p. 131), and cites in support of this the increased enthusiasm for dancing in war-time, and in the time of post-war social upheaval, or in adolescence, the period of great personal tension. If this is so, we may consider dance in a typical entertainment programme as 'managing' the tensions inherent in our social structure and activity. It follows that *Come Dancing* would appear to meet a relatively stable and enduring set of needs for it has been on British screens in much the same form for the last twenty-five years. The programme is essentially a dancing match between two teams representing regions of Britain. Each team provides one couple for each of six different dances – rumba and jive, tango and military twostep, waltz and quickstep. In addition there are two team events – novelty dancing and formation dancing.

If dancing in real life is a ritual based on both normal social behaviour and more abstract socio-cultural influences, then *Come Dancing* adds to it the ritual of sport. For sport is conflict enacted, structured and concluded in a way that signifies many of the tensions in everyday life. Real-life conflict is rarely cleanly resolved, its uncertainties rarely answered, but sport provides these missing satisfactions by exploiting and formalizing uncertainty, and then resolving it; and the resolution, as we shall see later, is typically presented in terms of achievement.

In both sport and dance the relationship of performer to spectator is blurred; sometimes the spectator participates in the ritual by proxy, sometimes he is asked to sit back and evaluate objectively. In *Come Dancing* what strikes us first is the participatory role of the audience: its members, as potential dancers, are represented formally by the dancers on the floor. The performers take to the floor from among the audience, and in some programmes the spectators actually dance before the cameras. The amateur status of the performers is stressed, typically by detailing their jobs, their home towns and ages, giving them a physical and class base where their daily lives, as opposed to their night-time dancing, take place.

So we are constantly invited to refer the ritual of *Come Dancing* back to pre-coded everyday life, but we are also expected to refer it out to other rituals – to the ritualized conflict of sport, of beauty competitions, of fashion parades and of professional spectacular dance. Beauty queens are frequently employed to keep the score, copious comments on the dancers' dresses are provided, performers' previous successes in competitions are given and there are constant references to professional dancing, particularly in the novelty dancing section which is an amateur version of the sort of modern dance frequently seen on light entertainment shows. The professional dancers on the light entertainment shows provide a goal for the amateurs, not only in their skill, but also, as professionals on television, in their culturally recognized bardic role.

But the programme is basically composed of two main codes which operate beneath the surface on the mythological level; these are sport as ritualized social conflict and dance as ritualized social coherence. The code of sport uses signs of comparison and evaluation of performance, here in the form of judges and their score cards, and of differentiation of self from other by the frequently stressed geographical base of each team. In other sports dress is used to differentiate but here, significantly, the dress of each team, like their behaviour, reflects their similarity, and is part of the code of social coherence.

The signs in television are like the words in language in that they can be members of a variety of sub-codes or registers, which indicate the breadth of their usefulness to the culture. Our discussion of television's bardic function has indicated some of the ways in which this usefulness may be achieved. It can reassure us as members of a culture that our ways of codifying pre-cultural reality, of organizing and understanding it, are adequate, or, to put it another way, that our ways of seeing and structuring this reality actually work. It can also reassure us that other members of the culture share our ways of seeing, share our ways of encoding reality. By using these codes and demonstrating that they are widely shared throughout the culture, television is contributing significantly to the maintenance of our cultural identity. When we watch a popular television programme we are, among other things, asserting our commonality with the other members of our culture.

So when the television screen gives a sign of three judges, each showing a numbered card indicating his evaluation of a dance out of 5, this simple and instantly decodable sign is part of a complex cultural process. For television provides ample evidence that our culture feels a need to rank people in order, either by physical or mental activity, or by appearance; the way of evaluating the competitors and of finding the winner is usually in numerical terms – the score. In this, television is doing no more than reflecting the competitive, hierarchical structure of our culture and the extent to which we use quantitative codes to evaluate, assess and describe our social activities. (It is almost impossible to imagine an Elizabethan describing a dancer's performance as 4 out of 5: he would turn to analogy rather than numbers, and might evaluate the dance by likening it to the movement of a bird, deer, horse, ox or pig.)

Come Dancing, then, offers a message at the cultural level that we are members of a competitive, hierarchical society. One would expect such a message to contain other codes by which this cultural characteristic is expressed, so it is not surprising to find that dress and behavioural codes are also representations of the class system that is the most central expression of this hierarchical, competitive principle.

The signs, again, are simple: they are of present-day, ordinary people using codes of dress and behaviour of a higher class of a different period, yet using them in such a way as to assert their contemporaneity and ordinariness. What we are viewing here is an enactment of the same myth to which the Cinderella fable appeals: that class differences are merely superficial ones of appearance and behaviour. This, of course, makes class mobility a matter of performance, which in turn enables us to reconcile one of our culture's central paradoxes: the maintenance of a relatively stable class system with a competitive ideology. But no one really believes that our class system is based on factors as simple as dress and behaviour, and so it is in *Come Dancing*. The codes are used 'in inverted commas', the dancers are using a form of behavioural irony by appearing to act as one class while really belonging to another.

Except when dancing the jive and the rumba, the men wear white tie and tails with white gloves, and carry themselves in a particular shoulders-back-and-head-up sort of posture while using arm, hand and leg movements that are ritualizations of the courtesy of the Edwardian upper class. The artificiality of these codes prevents them being totally convincing: we know, and the dancers know, that they are ordinary people from today's subordinate class. The women make this clear: their dresses have the opulence of those of the class they are 'imitating', but bring to it a brash 'vulgarity' in the quantity of petticoats and sequins, and in the stridency of the colours – all of which clearly asserts that they are not what they appear to be pretending to be.

The dances, too, reflect this quality of conscious self-deception. For they are formalizations of the dances traditionally performed in ordinary social life. They are so clearly rehearsed that the spontaneity of, say, a real quickstep has disappeared. The dance here is closer to pure form, the ritual element is intensified and the personal decreased. One effect of this, at least, is to desexualize the dance. Relationships between the couple are formal and are expressed in unity of movement, particularly circular movement; for that, according to Lange (1975), is the dance movement that expresses social unity and coherence. The relationship, though based on sex difference, is not sexual but one of social harmony.

The most contemporary, though still old-fashioned, dance performed, the Jive, is self-consciously ritualized away from the real dance into how-the-Edwardian-upper-class-would-have-danced-it-had-they-done-so, and is thus removed from its lower-class origin so that the working class can once again pretend to dance it.

The programme as a whole reflects a constant tension between realism and fantasy in terms of the class structure of our society; there is a deliberate indulgence in a fantasy that exaggerates its ability to provide an escape from the bonds of class and, to a lesser extent, of time. Yet the fact that the fantasy is deliberate negates it. While satisfying the needs for escape, the programme constantly refers back to reality. We, and the dancers, know that the clock will strike twelve, and they will return to the real world. This knowledge that the fantasy is both true and false, that the workers can and cannot become the bosses, and that elegance and glamour can and cannot exist in the streets of Bradford is derived from the semiotic irony that pervades the programme.

Ambivalence is apparent at all levels, even down to the detailed stylistics. The commentary and the camera complement each other. Sometimes the visual denotes and the verbal connotes, as when Terry Wogan uses words to signal the warmth of the spectators and to associate it with the glamour of the ballroom, and thus to connote the class-based reality/fantasy movement of the programme. Sometimes, however, the visual sign is connotative and the verbal denotative. In the slow tango, for instance, the dancing couple is held in a spotlight in the darkened ballroom. They are in a self-contained fantasy world, and the camera slides to their shadows dancing in a pool of light on the floor. Yet the commentary is giving us mundane facts about the couple, locating them and making the dress real by telling us of what and how it was made.

Dance, little lady

Come Dancing is not the normal dance on television – for that we must turn to the staged spectacular dance where the audience is less involved, where the skill of the performers is taken for granted and where the emphasis is therefore shifted to the signification of their performance. The spectators will undoubtedly find some aesthetic satisfaction in the dance, but the way it is presented suggests that aesthetics are only a minor consideration in the audience's reasons for viewing. For television spectacular dance is, in aesthetic terms, impoverished. The dancers use a *restricted code* of body position, the syntagmatic flow is likewise simplified and repetitious, and the time allowed is short, rarely exceeding five minutes. The dance is often not the focus of attention, but is blended with music and song, largely to increase the all-important variety of presentation, that is variety in the signifiers, while maintaining a restricted number of signifieds. Our study of *Come Dancing* has already indicated the underlying themes of class and sexual relationships, and it is the social tensions arising from these problem areas that are, we suggest, the ones managed by television dance.

We take, as typical examples, a glossy variety programme, *The Shirley Bassey Show*, and one aimed at a younger audience, *Top of the Pops*. Both were transmitted in the week beginning 15 November 1976.

The Shirley Bassey Show opens with the song 'Diamonds are a Girl's Best Friend'. The opening shot shows Shirley Bassey, dressed in an ankle-length mink coat arriving with her chauffeur at Cartier's, the Royal jewellers, in Bond Street. But they arrive on a tandem. During the song, Shirley Bassey, dressed in a long, slinky gown, low cut and slit to the top of one thigh, glides sexily around the shop admiring the jewellery. Finally, she picks up a handful of loose diamonds worth, according to the publicity, £250,000, and casually pours them from hand to hand as she sings. There is then a cut to 'Razzle Dazzle 'em', a studio song and dance number in which she is accompanied by a troupe of traditional music-hall dancers, the girls in high heels, fishnet tights, spangled leotards and plumed, spangled headdresses, the men in white tail suits, with white top hats and gloves, again liberally spangled.

The sexuality of both numbers is made plain, mainly in the costumes but also in the movements. Shirley Bassey's dress is sexy in a smart, fashionable style, though the height of the slit and the depth of the neckline show that it is a stage version of an evening gown rather than the real-life dress. In the 'spangles' number, the fish-net tights and the leotards emphasize the crutch, and the high heels throw the bottom out and exaggerate the length of leg. This is a sign of sexuality derived partly from the traditional high heels of the tart, but made acceptable in the dance by association with the legitimate points of the ballet dancer, for in ballet the legs of a female dancer are traditionally displayed for aesthetic, not sexual, pleasure.

The movements in the *elaborated code* of ballet are so far refined towards aesthetic form that their origins in courtly gesture and the art of swordplay have been left far behind; in the restricted code of stage dance, however, the loose-hipped, swinging walk which is its basic step, is still closely related to the negro walk and its evolution to dance through the jazz brothels of New Orleans (just as the music shows the jazz influence and the same evolution). The spangles are a *metaphoric* sign of diamonds and wealth, which, in their turn, are a sign, this time *metonymic*, of social success; in the dance these signs are combined with an overtly sexual movement that derives from the lower strata of society. Semiotically the dance is a sign of class tension and a signifier of the myth of upward class mobility, this time through female sexuality and not, as in *Come Dancing*, through dress and manner.

This linking of sexuality with social mobility is normal in our culture, where the woman sleeping or marrying her way up the social ladder is a common motif. Indeed, the glamour of showbiz with its vulgarity and ostentation is a popular cultural sign precisely because it signifies the social acclaim with which our society rewards ability, yet distinguishes between the *nouveau riche* and the genuine article. This takes us back to the 'Diamonds' number, when the joky opening on the tandem is a self-parodying sign of the working-class origins of the star and a reminder that she still retains her roots there. Similarly, the ostentatious sexuality of the bourgeois-derived gown also signifies the class mobility myth. Members of our culture find their fantasy needs satisfied and class-sexual tensions structured through this form of dance. It is located in the music-hall tradition of working-class, urban culture, which has constantly relieved the frustrations of those trapped at the bottom of the class system. For working-class entertainers appeared in the gowns, parasols and dress suits of the bourgeoisie, and even as the well-dressed, well-spoken but down-and-out 'faded beau'.

The spectacular dance of television also enacts and structures sexual tension. By making the sexuality of the moving female body public, well lit and open, it legitimizes our society's view of the female as a sex-object, and while implying her availability to the male, also relieves him of the potential responsibility and/or guilt of a merely sexual relationship. The safety of the sexuality is increased by the plurality of the dancers: sex is no longer private, no longer the responsibility of the individual (notice that a striptease is usually solo, and even when two or more strippers take part, they dance individually, not in unison). But the plurality is more than this, for if, as Lange (1975) asserts, dancing in unison is a metaphor of social unity, then the dance of sexual display 'naturalizes' our view of women as sex-objects by showing it to be part of the social structure and thus acceptable on the fireside screen.

The acceptability of this sexual display derives from the co-existence of a number of socially based codes. First, as we have seen, there is the plurality of the dancers which becomes a metaphor for social harmony and acceptability; then there is their dress which refers to the showbiz-star system and its associations with sexuality, social success and class mobility. These codes operate within the more formal aesthetic (and thus legitimizing) codes seen in the beauty of gesture, movement and grouping in the syntagmatic form of the dance, and in its expression, through its relationship with the song, of concerns that are central to our popular culture. This combination of codes allows different audiences to decode the screen image selectively paying more or less attention to various parts of the composite whole, and thus to arrive at a personal decoding that is *aberrant*. By this term we mean that the message is individually decoded, but still retains a broad generality of meaning which makes it a popular cultural experience. To put it simply, Mum and Dad will each find different, though overlapping, parts of the dance to enjoy, though their enjoyment will, ultimately, be shared.

This potential for aberrant decoding is one of the characteristics of *broadcast* codes as opposed to *narrowcast* ones. Striptease, or classical Indian hand-dancing, for example, are narrowcast dances which aim at sending a defined message to a defined audience, and are therefore not well suited to television as a medium.

A Hard Day's Night

But even the 'broadcast' codes of television can, and do, appeal to a defined audience: not all its programmes are aimed at the heterogeneous mass of viewers. The all-female Legs and Co., the dancers on *Top of the Pops*, dance for a specific audience, an adolescent one, whose members may see themselves as part of a dislocated subculture which is outside the class structure of central society. Rust (1969) writes:

> The ultimate in democratic dance forms has perhaps been reached with contemporary 'modern beat' dancing. Here the only barrier is that of age group. Since no special style has to be learnt, and no particular steps have been handed down by tradition, young people of widely varying background, experience and education can join in freely if they wish. (p. 128)

So for them the tensions of class are less insistent, the crucial ones are those of identity and relationship. Of course, this dance performed for them, like the dances they perform, may eventually move into socio-centrality, and will then be available for a culturally central programme like *Come Dancing*. Again, the dance itself is simple, its kinesic and proxemic codes (those of movement and of space) are restricted, but its relationship to its audience is much closer. The dance is performed on the studio floor in the centre of the studio audience, and is a professionalization of their own disco dances; indeed, at the end of the dance, the young audience joins in with a technique not much inferior to that of the professionals.

Despite the specificity of its immediate audience this type of dance fits a 'broadcast' medium better than, say, the Indian hand-dance would, not just because of the range of codes it uses, but because of the restriction of each code within that range. The gestures, body positions and movements of the dancers are limited as are the spatial relations of the dancers to each other, the groupings and patterns they form. The elaborated codes of the Indian hand-dance, or of classical ballet, require an audience experienced in decoding them, a subculture of taste defined by its decoding ability, that will be more homogeneous and specific than that typically reached by a 'broadcast' medium.

Where television has to deal with an elaborated, narrowcast code, such as in ballet, it is frequently content merely to transmit the stage version. Where it tries to exploit its potential as a medium and to mediate classical ballet, or music, in the hope of reaching a wider audience, it usually manages only to offend the purists, and lay itself open to the charge of distracting from or even distorting the aesthetic effect of the original. Striptease, of course, is unsuitable for broadcasting because it lacks social legitimation: indeed, its illegitimacy is crucial to its effect.

Although Legs and Co. dance for a specific and dislocated subculture, we may expect, from the fact that their dance is 'broadcast', that it will be legitimate, that it will employ a range of restricted codes and that it will therefore be available to a wider audience than its original target one. This is borne out by an analysis of the dance. Legs and Co. are dressed in spangled bikinis whose sexuality is legitimized by pretty strips of 'romantic' chiffon which join hip and wrist but actually conceal nothing. They are skimpy metonyms of flowing robes, or of the long dresses of *Come Dancing*. The dance is overtly sexual; hip, stomach and thigh movements are its base, the girls are barefoot and their long hair swings to their movements (this is significantly opposed to the controlled hair of the dancers in *Come Dancing* or *The Shirley Bassey Show*, and is, semiotically, a 'distinctive feature').

The proxemic signs are based on the circle, but it is a static one, for the girls dance each on one spot, though grouped in a circle, or else move towards and away from the focus, each on her own radius. This is significant, for the circle connotes social harmony, and was one of the basic movements in *Come Dancing*, as the couples circled both round each other and the floor. But it is clearly less appropriate as a basic form for a dance of a dislocated subculture. So the Legs and Co. dance is, in fact, individualistic. While based on the circle, the girls dance individually, like disco dancers. They relate to each other by a common rhythm and common restricted dance vocabulary, but concentrate primarily on their own dance experience rather than on a relationship. This form of dance seems to reflect the tensions caused by the identity and sexual crises of adolescence. Dance is particularly useful in this culture, in that it can relieve both identity and sexual tensions without recourse to actual relationships.

What this dance *signifies* then, in the first order, is the sexuality and culturally defined beauty of the female body. In the second order it *connotes* the adolescent concern with identity alongside its concern with sexuality; the movement into and away from the circle's focus becomes a connotative signifier of the adolescents' ambivalent attitudes to society, and their problems in resolving the clash between the demands of their own personalities and those of others or of the society to which they have to adjust. But the satisfaction for the audience, particularly the participating studio audience, lies in the fact that the dance gives form to this anarchic source of feelings about identity/sexuality, and thus asserts that these feelings can be both shaped and controlled in a way that in real life they may not be. But we must remember that while these feelings impinge on the individual, they are, in fact, social: that is, they are located in, and partly define, the subculture of youth. The ritual of dance is not a form of psychotherapy for the individual, for what it offers is effective for him only in so far as it binds him into his subculture. In this, the dance of Legs and Co. is similar to that of the Shirley Bassey troupe, in that both provide satisfying entertainment by their ability to make the tensions of the individual communal and thus legitimate.

The three types of dancing we have seen formalize three different structures of sexual relationship. In *Come Dancing*, the ballroom dance reflects a social structure where male and female roles are clearly distinguished by dress, by manner, and by the fact that the male leads and the female follows. There is a sexual hierarchy as well as a class one. Rust (1969) contrasts this type of sex-differentiated dancing with indiscriminate dancing where males and females dance either together or separately in single- or mixed-sex groups. This latter type of dancing is typical of cultures with outspoken and direct attitudes to sexuality, which often goes with a weak differentiation of sex roles, and, we might suggest, with an unmarked class structure. The contemporary disco dance clearly comes into this category. So the female dancers of Legs and Co. do not need the presence of males to structure the sexuality of the subculture for which they are performing, with its minimized differentiation of sex roles. Sexuality here is individual sexuality, and not, as in *Come Dancing*, a function of a social role. A social role, we note, can be defined only by contrast with another – in the case of *Come Dancing*, the role of the opposite sex.

The spectacular dancers of *The Shirley Bassey Show* come between these two extremes, but they are closer to *Come Dancing* in that the sex differentiation is marked, though dancers do not dance in couples. Sometimes the women dance as a group, sometimes the men do, and sometimes the two single-sex groups dance together. The sexuality is not of the individual, nor of the private relationship, but of a public, socially validated kind, and associated through the semiotics of the dress with the class system. The 'spectacular dance' differentiates sex roles and refers to the class system, while the disco dance of Legs and Co. does the opposite, but both are an example of 'tension management' for different age groups or subcultures of our society.

Despite their fundamental similarity of function, the two stage dances have significant differences, the most obvious being that of the style by which they are televised. The Shirley Bassey number is presented conventionally, alternating between mid-shot and long-shot with no effect more exceptional than one shot by a camera looking down on the dance at about a forty-five-degree angle. The dance and its presentation are traditional, not to say old-fashioned, and it may be that one of the reasons for the relative unpopularity of the show was its failure to link the traditional form of its content directly to the contemporary situation of its audience.

Legs and Co., on the other hand, are presented in a way that deviates markedly from the norms of television in general, but conforms to the norms of the programme *Top of the Pops*. Electronic effects, colour distortion, odd camera angles are employed, sometimes to reinforce the significance of the dance, but sometimes to distinguish stylistically between this programme and the rest of television output, for this programme is aimed at the audience who uses television least, and who will thus respond best to a programme that dissociates itself from the mainstream. A shot that illustrates the way in which effects can reinforce the dance is one in which a long-shot of one of the girls dancing is superimposed upon a close-up of another girl's navel as she performs the same dance. The shot connotes both the off-beat sexuality of the dance itself and the inward-turned, hallucinatory, dislocated characteristics of the youth culture.

Come Dancing and the Shirley Bassey number both emit conventional messages operating within the cultural centrality of our class-based society. The Legs and Co. message decentralizes itself by signalling clearly and self-consciously that it is non-traditional, non-bourgeois. It can therefore achieve its effect only in opposition to those which, like *Come Dancing* and *The Shirley Bassey Show*, comprise the mainstream of television output. But its decentrality is moderated by the fact that it is a *television* message, and television is a culturally central medium: the really dislocated subcultures do not feature in the broadcast communication system at all. *Top of the Pops* represents the most legitimated, acceptable aspect of youth culture.

10 COMPETITION

Boy meets goal

IN terms of the television message, the distance between dancing and sport is not great: the difference lies mainly between the signifiers. The signifieds are located in the same cultural area, in that both involve the ritualization and evaluation of social behaviour. A typical television sports programme is *Match of the Day*, which consists of recorded highlights of one or two of the afternoon's football games, presented from the studio by the expert, Jimmy Hill. The recordings are completed by interviews with players and/or managers.

Like *Come Dancing*, the programme is a second-stage structure of reality. As *Come Dancing* is a formalization of dance, which is itself formalized behaviour, so *Match of the Day* is a re-presentation of sport, which is itself ritualized behaviour. The second stage of this signification process clarifies and foregrounds what the television producers interpret as the culturally central motifs of the first. Just as out of the many potential functions of dance, *Come Dancing* spotlights a few and ignores others (such as sexual relationships), so, of the many functions of sport, *Match of the Day* concentrates on signifying achievement through conflict.

For the spectator, the main appeal of sport lies in the way it exploits and then resolves uncertainty: the game is 'about' achievement and winning. In America winning appears to rank even higher in the cultural value system than in Britain: 'Football in the USA continues to become a whole different ball game. Americans like a winner. "Playing to a tie", says one coach "is like kissing your sister." So the game must have a tie breaker' (*The Sunday Times*, November 1976). Television, however, modifies any cultural activity: the experience of dancing is not what *Come Dancing* communicates, nor does *Match of the Day* communicate the experience of watching live sport. Signs about a reality, even if that reality is itself a symbolic one, do not reproduce it, but add another stage of cultural mediation to our perceptual/interpretive process.

So *Match of the Day* is about achievement, and the sign of achievement is a goal (the full meaning of the word should not be missed). In the early evening trailers for the programme, the BBC frequently quotes the number of goals as the main attraction: 'And in Match of the Day at 10 p.m. we have seven goals.' The programme on 18 September 1976 was introduced as containing the 'highest scoring match of the season', and one of the teams, York, was described as not yet having scored a goal away from home.

The form of the presentation, of course, supports this theme. In this particular match there were nine goals: eight of them were re-presented in the same way:

Shot 1 A middle distance shot, from a height, of the goal being scored.

Shot 2 A close-up, ground level shot of the scorer, showing his triumphant expression and gestures.

Shot 3 A quick shot of the beaten goalkeeper.

Shot 4 A shot of the scorer receiving the congratulations of his team-mates.

Shot 5 A shot from ground level, of the cheering fans above, as the scorer is experiencing them.

This achievement syntagm culminates in a slow-motion savouring of the goal being scored (*Shot 6*) and of the initial triumph of the scorer. The syntagm celebrates achievement, personal satisfaction and cultural acclaim and, only to a lesser extent, victory over a defeated opponent.

So television does not merely bring raw sport into our home, it uses sport as a code to converse with us about aspects of our individual/cultural values. But we do not only participate by proxy, for the evaluative comments of Jimmy Hill require us to make a crucial shift of viewpoint, to that of evaluator. The original binary criterion of goal/no goal now becomes a graduated scale of 'how good'. Jimmy Hill does not actually mark each goal out of 5, but he does bring to our perception of it this mode of evaluation – objective, analytic and 'knowing'. Our shift from participant to judge is crucial in the cultural role of the programme.

The after-match interview with the manager of the winning team enacts this dual role for us. The achievements of the players are his, and his satisfaction is the same as theirs; yet he also comments on and evaluates their performances, as do we, the armchair judges. Sometimes the interview is with a player, as it is after the second match in this programme, but the change in signifier is not matched by a change in signified; the player relives his satisfaction in scoring, but also evaluates his achievement. So the home viewer has his position enacted and justified by the participants: the satisfaction is dual – the status of being in the know with the experts and of being an achiever with the participants.

This appears to be a particularly satisfying format for sports programmes: *Rugby Special*, screened the following day, has also adopted it. The game's highlights, with a similar 'achievement syntagm' (except for the omission of the defeated opponent motif), are followed by an after-match interview of much the same type.

After the match highlights, *Match of the Day* has the sports news, in which the headlines are not the results of the games, but the main goal-scorers of the day. The programme also runs a 'goal of the month' competition, in which the viewer is asked to rank a number of goals in order of merit; the evaluative skill of the viewer is then evaluated by yet another expert.

The programme's emphasis on achievement must not blind us to the fact that the achievement results from conflict Conflict is ritualized, through the rules, into possession of and progression with the ball. But rules can be broken, and real conflict can erupt out of the rituals in the form of blows traded between opposing players. It is at this point that the television mediation of sport becomes most intrusive. It foregrounds the non-partisan, evaluative aspects of the game, inviting us, especially through the mediating commentary, to perceive it 'objectively'. So television sport differs from sport itself in rejecting as 'unsportsmanlike' the more physical manifestations of competitive conflict. However, the effect of this is for television sport to propose a preferred meaning for its subject, one which happens to coincide with what we have earlier described as the dominant meaning system. In other words, the glorification of the goal in the abstract, the objective evaluation of games which serve almost as texts for analysis, and the denial of the actual spectators' subjective, partisan, class- and locality-based experience of the game turn television football into an attempted transformation of oral (working-class) modes into literate (bourgeois) ones.

In short, *Match of the Day* is not football, in the way that *Come Dancing* is not dancing. Both programmes offer, in the ritual that is their subject, evidence of activities that are more widespread in the culture than are the first-stage ritualizations of them. There is a broader audience for the television programme than for the actual activity itself, and this difference is reflected in the 'distortion' of the subject-matter. For Jimmy Hill, in his role as bard, has pulled the game further to the centre of our value system and has thus legitimized it for a wider audience.

Television offers a large number of programmes of this competition-conflict type. These range from live sports broadcasts, sports news and comment programmes, through beauty competitions and sheepdog trials, to quizzes and game shows. Indeed, in an average week some 16 per cent of viewing hours comprise this sort of programme. What they all have in common is a two-dimensional structure of relationships:

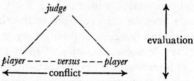

The horizontal relationships between player and player are expressed in terms of a conflict governed by a set of rules designed to ensure both equality of opportunity for all players and a measurable result. In this relationship the viewer is invited to participate by proxy and thus to achieve a conscious result (either winning or losing) in a way that is usually not possible in the less formally structured conflicts of everyday life.

The vertical relationship, that of evaluation, invites the viewer to recognize his real, as opposed to his proxy situation. He is here *not* a participant and so is objective enough to be an evaluator. The viewer is invited to share the high status role of judge, and in this, to involve his real and culturally valued faculties of discrimination and assessment. The judges' cards in *Come Dancing* are a cultural sign, and a validation of the process the viewer has gone through: the judge enacts our discriminatory powers as does the football analyst-expert.

In quiz shows, too, we are invited to share the roles of both judge and players, but an important difference here is that status is conferred by knowledge, not ability. In all societies, knowledge or information is a source of power, and the withholding or granting of it a common method of patronage. In quiz shows, the social value of information is ritualized into a form where it can be quantified and thus assessed in a competitive format. The question-master combines the roles of referee in the game and evaluator-expert in the studio: his relationship with the players operates both within the ritual of the game itself, and in the assessment by which the game is related to real life. The assessment relates the closed system of the game to the open system of life, in terms of how much real-life knowledge the player has, and how he can employ it in the quiz format. In all competitive programmes, the vertical relationships involve the bringing of real-life abilities or knowledge to the ritualized conflict: this involves both axes of the diagram, and the consequent celebration of each in terms of the other is one function of the bard.

Didn't he do well?

A show with a different sort of bard, but one which still uses the device of competition to test performances and value systems is *The Generation Game*, a popular quiz/game show on BBC. More explicitly than in *Come Dancing*, the competition is presented as entertainment, and the competitiveness played down. In the quizzes and games the score is of less importance than the entertainment they provide. Kuehn (1976) has shown how American quiz-show contestants consciously adopt showbiz norms. The prizes are valuable, and there is a real competitiveness, but still the showbiz norms of 'putting oneself over well' or 'projecting a good image' override the desire to win, as though being good on television is more important than being good at quizzes. In practice, of course, there is no clash, as the seasoned contestants – many of whom are semi-professional – know that their chances of being selected for further shows, and thus their chances of making more money, depend on their showbiz abilities.

In this British show the prizes are comparatively small:

the winner gets about twenty consumer durables whose values range from some £2 to perhaps £25. This reduces further the competitive element, and the compère/question-master, Bruce Forsyth, constantly emphasizes the fun it all is – 'bit o' fun' is one of his catchphrases. While doubtless part of the reason for entering the show is the hope of winning, at least an equal motive is the desire to be on television, and thus to be an active cultural agent at the transmitting rather than the receiving sector of the communication circle.

In effect, the programme is communicating, through the televisual codes of competition and entertainment, a series of norms and values located in showbiz and the family, in such a way as to legitimize each by the closeness of its fit with the other. This reciprocal legitimation, which only works because of the widespread acceptance of each value system, results in fact from a circular argument. We know the family norms are right because they fit so well with the showbiz norms and so on.

If we look at a typical programme in more detail, we can see this in practice. The games are played between pairs of contestants from one family, and each is of a different generation and sex. Thus, in the show transmitted on 9 October 1976 there were two father/daughter pairs, one aunt/nephew and one mother/son. The younger generation are always in their late teens to early twenties, and the older in middle age. Each pair is introduced by Bruce Forsyth giving details of how the contestant met his/her spouse, their jobs, hobbies, social activities, where they went for their holidays and, crucially, something funny that has recently happened to them. They are identified as representative of typical families, and are asked to relate to Bruce Forsyth as the jolly uncle. He is *familiar*, in the root sense of the word, calls them 'my love', and uses the codes of touch and space to establish this familiarity: he often hugs them in a non-sexual familial way, and stands close to them, inside that proximity normally reserved for intimates.

This jolly uncle role fits well with his music-hall compère

role, for both are concerned to externalize and reinforce social relationships, whether between members of a family or between audience and performer. The essential family norm of 'getting on well together' in an explicit, extroverted way is close to the showbiz norm of 'projecting oneself well', that is, of communicating a warmth of personality that will draw the audience into a secure relationship with the performer. In this sense, both music-hall star and family member are meeting the need of dependence, the need of security, approval and acceptance. It is noticeable, too, that the style of the programme – vulgar, loud, familiar – the norms of family closeness, and the code of the music-hall tradition, are all located in the working-class cultural tradition. Middle-class reticence and good taste are inappropriate here. It is in this firm location in the working-class value system that the music-hall norms and the family norms merge and validate each other.

Bruce Forsyth himself plays a crucial role in bringing the norms together, for he embodies the values common to both systems. He projects his love of the audience to elicit theirs, and thus to enable himself to act as a social catalyst through whom people can express their satisfaction in having a good time in the company of others. Shared enjoyment is one of the strongest cultural cohesives, and Bruce Forsyth continually foregrounds it: 'Hope you did well at home with that', he says, 'it's a good game, bit o' fun', and he gestures for the enthusiastic applause that the studio audience readily gives him.

The norms, of course, are in practice impossible to separate from the codes that embody them, for both are interdependent elements in the culture. The games through which the families compete have their roots in the party games of the family celebration, in which the competitive element provides the form but not the substance. They are usually of two sorts: the first a knowledge-testing, pencil and paper game, and the second an activity involving skill or dexterity. Typical of the first are identifying television comedians by their catchphrases, naming a number of house plants or linking signature tunes with their programmes; typical of the activities are serving spaghetti, making a bowl on a potter's wheel or decorating a cake with icing.

In the pencil and paper games, which normally relate their content to the home or to television, the answers are marked by Bruce Forsyth and his glamorous assistant, Anthea Redfern. They give fulsome praise to correct answers, and dwell on funny wrong ones. In the activity games, the activity is demonstrated by a professional or expert and the contestants copy him. The expert then marks their attempts. Again the camera dwells longest on those who are failing most funnily. The expert is significantly introduced as a 'special guest', but he is not an expert in the sense that Jimmy Hill is, or the judges in *Come Dancing*, for his distance from the layman is minimized. Indeed, he is the only evaluator who performs the activity he is evaluating and who expects the contestants (or audience-by-proxy) to copy him. Though he can perform the activity better, the difference is one of degree, not of kind. The comic failure of the competitors binds them to the audience and is thus legitimized. Indeed, one of the main functions of the programme is to legitimize failure and to assert that it is not necessarily evidence of inadequacy. Bruce Forsyth has another catchphrase which emphasizes this: 'Isn't he doing well?' he says, particularly when a contestant is not.

American game shows are far less kind to the loser. Many exploit the emotional yo-yo between the elation of winning and the despair of losing: cameras dwell in long close-up upon the faces of contestants and their emotions – one contestant who wanted a car in *The Price is Right* was reduced to gibbering with greed, the camera closed up on him, the compère taunted him; drawing out his anticipation. In *Let's Make a Deal* a typical sequence illustrates this. The contestant, a middle-aged overweight lady, is faced with thirty boxes, in one of which is a cheque for $25,000. She chooses a box, the compère clowns suspense as he slowly opens it and finds in it a piece of paper . . . which turns out to be a token valid for one tyre (close-up of hope); 'over there . . . a uni-cycle, worth \$14.95' (close-up of disappointment). 'Would you', he goes on, 'like to trade that tyre for two tyres, and whatever is attached them?' She agrees and gets a bicycle worth \$42.50. Her face registers resignation, a determined cheerfulness, and she leaves the stage, only to be called back at the last moment and offered the opportunity to trade those two tyres for four. (Close-up of real hope.) Her voice is cracking as she accepts. Four men immediately rush on and tie her up with ribbons: they, it transpires, are the 'ti-ers'. Her despair has now reduced her almost to tears, and again the camera closes up on her tightened face. 'But really', says the compère, 'the tyres are on this', and the curtains open to reveal a 1937 Rolls Royce worth \$11,147. She collapses.

The difference between *Let's Make a Deal* and *The Generation Game* points us to the harsher competitiveness of American society, and the sequence above may be seen as a syntagm of free enterprise, with the emphasis on the risk-taking, get-rich-quick version, rather than on the more sober old-fashioned one of hard work being the recipe for success. This show certainly does not validate failure, rather it vilifies it, and in so doing reinforces the society's lack of concern for the loser or underdog. Much the same sort of difference between American and British shows and social values appears in the family codes as well. *The Generation Game* and other British quiz shows like *Ask the Family* or *Mr and Mrs* emphasize and reward the unity and teamwork of the family members, whereas the American show, *The Newlyweds*, rewards the newly married couple who have the best fights and misunderstandings. The competing couples are told before the show to 'play rough and dirty' with each other. It can be no coincidence that this is a popular show in a society with a high divorce rate, for it underlies the view of marriage as domestic conflict, and thus has a realism that its many critics ignore.

But let us return to *The Generation Game*. After each of the two early games the score is totalled, and the two winning pairs go forward to the semi-final. This next game brings together explicitly the family and entertainment norms, and is based on the structured opposition of professional/layman. Here, the professionals are actors who enact a short sketch in which the contestants then have to take key roles. Their performances are marked by the professionals. Bruce Forsyth, too, acts in the sketch and mediates between the amateurs and professionals. The sketch thus brings together the competition and music-hall codes, but before we look at it in greater detail we must take a closer look at the way the music-hall code is established in the earlier part of the programme.

Bruce Forsyth brings with him his past context, that of compère of *Sunday Night at the London Palladium*, one of television's most successful variety shows. In terms of television language he is a sign, and like any other, brings to the present use the cultural accumulations of past usages. The title of the show is given in the style of an old music-hall bill, and the opening shot shows Forsyth on a television variety stage in a pose that has become his trademark. He then comes towards the audience, welcoming them with his catchphrase 'Nice to see you, to see you ...', and the audience roars back 'Nice!'. He introduces Anthea Redfern (the hostess whom he has married with much publicity during the run of the programme), emphasizes her glamour by admiring her dress, and the two then go into an exaggerated comedy routine:

Anthea: What sea has waves, but no water?
Bruce: What sea has waves, but no water? I don't know Anthea, tell me, what sea has waves, but no water?
Anthea: The BBC!
Bruce: The BBC, oh that's clever, that is!

The music-hall code is thus established at the start. Its

norms and those of the family are, however, made to con-
verge by Bruce Forsyth's ambivalent role, as both compère
and 'jolly uncle'. He wears not the stage costume of a compère, but an ordinary everyday suit that will enable him to
relate visually to the contestants when they appear. In
addition we are told that this comedy routine was sent in by
a family viewer, whose name, address and (young) age are
given.

Bruce Forsyth continually verbalizes his role, and that of
the contestants, as one of 'being on television'. He does it not
only by the normal address to the camera, and thus to the
viewer at home, but also by specific references, as when he
comments on a mistake: 'We'll cut that out, don't worry.'
Significantly, the editor cuts neither the mistake nor the
remark; this is acceptable because the programme legitimizes mistakes and celebrates being on television. Other
typical deliberate references to this televisual role are, for
instance (on a bad pun), 'Even the production staff are
getting restless'; or a comparison of himself with the disc
jockey Jimmy Young, 'He talks even faster than I do, I'm
sorry for the roof of his mouth – it must take a hammering
from his tongue'. This is all metalanguage (see above, p. 84).
As Barthes (1968) says: 'A metalanguage is a system whose
plane of content is itself constituted by a signifying system'.
In other words it is language which is about language.

The whole programme is, metalinguistically, about 'being
on television'. It exists solely for television, unlike *Match of
the Day* and *Come Dancing*, where television is presented as
being merely a channel (despite the addition of a televisual
significance to a pre-televisual or everyday reality). It is
constructed from the codes of the music-hall and of competition, which become, metalinguistically, the content of
the programme itself. All the various levels of signification
come together in the dramatic sketch that is the semi-final of
the competition.

The sketch here concerns Nell Gwyn trying to seduce
Charles II on a huge four-poster bed in the centre of the

stage. A sub-plot involves the chamberlain and a chamber-maid (and, inevitably, a chamberpot), in which seduction is again the subject of the humour. It also involves the chambermaid putting on the queen's crown, which enables Charles II to mistake her for his wife, and collapse at being discovered in a compromising situation. The sketch ends with the four characters forming a chorus line facing the audience, and singing and dancing to the tune of Nelly Dean.

The jokes are either good-natured and vulgar, exploiting the tension between sexuality and the constraints of family morality, or else they are farcical, based on the difference between the amateurs – how people really act (behave), and the professionals – how actors act (perform) on television. In the professional demonstration, the actors ham it up, that is, they exaggerate those aspects of the acting code that distinguish it from the behaviour it represents, and thus draw attention to the code as code. This is metalanguage again, in that the actor is acting an actor acting.

The contestants play the parts of Charles II and the chambermaid, and the difference in skill between them and the professionals emphasizes that they are at the same time both real people and enacted characters. As Nell Gwyn enters, she suddenly sees Charles and launches herself at him, knocks him backwards on to the bed and lies on top of him in an amorous struggle. When the first pair of contestants are performing, Charles is played by a handsome young student, and the actress playing Nell, together with Bruce Forsyth (the chamberlain) continually switch roles between being actors and being themselves in trying to stop him, as a young man really enjoying the amorous embrace, while encouraging him, as King Charles, to act his enjoyment. The comedy derives from the way that the one signifier can have two signifieds – one of a real young man, and one of King Charles II – and that they are simultaneously similar and different. In the second pair, Charles is played by a middle-aged man, slightly built, bespectacled and balding.

When Nell launches herself at him, he is embarrassed, and she has quite a struggle to steer him on to the bed, where he makes less than convincing gestures of enjoyment. The actress playing Nell signals her reality as a woman by laughing sympathetically at his embarrassment, before reverting to the amorous Nell and increasing it. The student Charles is a sign of the King in one code, and of the sexually active young male in the other; the middle-aged Charles is also a sign both of his real and of his stage role; Nell responds appropriately to each. In this one sign, then, there is explicit evidence of three codes, that of the normal family values, the comic sexuality of the music hall, and the metacode of being on television. There is also implicit evidence of the code of competitive evaluation, because we never forget the professionals' enactment of the scene, which provides the criterion of judgement.

This playlet is, in semiotic terms, the climax of the programme, even though it is only the semi-final of the competition. The final involves the winning pair competing against each other now, to see who goes for the main prize. There are three simple questions to answer. The winner then goes into a booth where, for 45 seconds, consumer durables pass before him on a conveyor belt. He has then 45 seconds to remember them, and keeps all that he remembers. Bruce Forsyth constantly jogs his memory – and encourages the studio audience to do the same – so that he does, in fact, 'remember' all or nearly all of them. It is only the form, not the substance, of a test. The competition that preceded it, too, is form rather than substance, in that the loser of the pair is necessarily in the same family as the winner, and the prizes are prizes for the family, not for the individual. There is no loser, no real failure. The competitive element exists more as a structuring device than as a substantial reality: it becomes a validation for the parade of family rewards for the pair who have best celebrated and reinforced the norms of the family and working-class entertainment upon which the programme is based.

These competition-based programmes form a distinct television genre that meets a definable set of socio-cultural needs, for genres in any medium develop and change to meet their audience's 'subculture' of taste. What is common to all texts in the genre should identify the centre of its audience's subcultural homogeneity. The programmes in this genre all, to put it simply, expose and then resolve conflict. The criteria by which winners are identified and evaluated may vary, but the process does not. The core 'needs' that this genre sets out to satisfy are thus discernible as those which underlie a free-enterprise, competitive, though liberal, society in which winners are rewarded, and losers protected, not humiliated. The class structure underlies the codes by which the programmes are presented on television, for society rewards its winners by movement up through the class system. These class-based codes reveal, however, an essentially binary simplification of the class system, into a culturally dominant class, and a dominated one. Part of the complexity of television is the way in which it articulates the social tensions formed by this opposition.

In *Come Dancing*, the myth of class mobility is structured into the programme, and it can be seen as a modern enactment of the Cinderella fable, though with the additional critical dimensions produced by the self-awareness of the enactors. Showbiz glamour and spectacular dance are, in their terms, similar fantasies of the accessibility of the bourgeois dominant role. *Match of the Day* is often described as a middle-class presentation of a working-class game. The communal involvement in attending a match and cheering on 'our side' is close to working-class norms of behaviour. On the other hand, the cool evaluation of *Match of the Day*, where we appraise skill and experience achievement, regardless of the identity of the team, is a more restrained, balanced, middle-class mode of perceiving the same cultural event. In these programmes the competition, where present, is real, as is the class tension.

In the *Generation Game*, however, the competition is a

formality and the class tensions pushed right to the background, for the bourgeois value system is there mainly in the material prizes, which are anyway subsumed into the working-class family value system that is the foundation of the programme. This loss of substance of the competitiveness may well signify the irrelevance of the values of a free-enterprise, competitive society to the norms of family or community life. *The Generation Game*, in its final effect, asserts the validity of non-competitive communal values within the structure of a competitive society, and is thus working within an area of cultural tension for which our society has not found a comfortable point of equilibrium.

So while the simple binary model of dominant/dominated may indicate the basis of our class structure, we must be chary of applying it too directly to the texts. A cultural text is always to a certain extent ambivalent. It never merely celebrates or reinforces a univalent set of culturally located attitudes, but rather reflects the tensions caused by the many contradictory factors that any culture is continually having to reconcile into a working equilibrium. Cultures are dynamic organisms, in continuous development, and television is active in this process. We are still a bourgeois society, but the dominance of the bourgeoisie is perhaps being challenged, the point of social equilibrium changing.

Television plays its part in this change, not only by its recognition of cultural tensions, but also by the way it is turning away from the literate cultural forms with which it started, towards alternative, often more effective, forms derived from working-class oral culture. In any process of derivation, of course, origins are obscured and transformed, but at least two important precursors of television discourse can be mentioned. The first is the circus and music-hall tradition, where despite a rapidly changing variety of signifiers, the signifieds exhibit genuine cultural homogeneity. The second is what may be called the folk-tale tradition, where recurrent motifs are of greater cultural significance than any single text in which they may occur.

Light entertainment inherits many characteristics (and some personnel) from the circus/music-hall tradition, while it may be argued that the police or hospital series inherit some of the characteristics and much of the appeal of the folk-tale. As a result we can see that television, whose place in society is much more central than that of any of the forms from which it is derived, brings to the forefront of our cultural stage the ephemeral verbal arts of a subordinate subculture. Television may not threaten the *fact* of dominant culture; but that culture's preferred literate modes of perception and representation have found a worthy and entertaining challenger.

11 TELEVISION REALISM

HITHERTO we have been stressing the degree to which television uses a constructed semiotic system to communicate culturally agreed, conventional meanings. If its signs are all artifice, and in the final analysis all arbitrary, how then does the world presented nightly on television appear to be so real?

In this chapter we shall attempt to show that there is no single answer to this question. Indeed, we argue that television's verisimilitude results from its exploitation of two different but simultaneously represented ways of constructing what we think of as reality. These two 'approaches' to reality on television derive ultimately from the two modes, oral and literate, that we described at the end of chapter 8. According to our analysis, literate modes generate the set of conventional devices known generally as *realism*, while oral modes generate a much less easily recognized or defined set of conventions which we shall introduce towards the end of this chapter.

We argued in chapter 8 that the television medium is characteristically oral rather than literate in its 'ways of seeing' reality. But it serves a society whose investment in the modes of thought associated with literacy is very great. Hence any purely formal relations between the literate-derived modes of realism and the oral-derived modes of television are crucially modified by the intervention of cultural choice. In other words, even if realism doesn't 'naturally' fit the oral television medium, our culture's dominant modes of perception will still force an entry.

As a result, television produces its version of reality by means of the intersection of these two contradictory modes. We can represent them schematically as follows

oral (*television*) modes

———————|——— literate (*dominant cultural*) modes
                      (*realism*)

We shall devote most of this chapter to a discussion of realism and its application to television. Later on we shall signpost one or two manifestations of what we have called television's oral modes, bearing in mind that many of those listed in chapter 8 (p. 124) figure in the following discussion only implicitly. For instance, part of television's 'dialectical' characteristic is to be discerned in the constant contradiction between the modes we are concerned with here. News is a good example of the dialectic in action, where 'journalistic' codes compete with a dramatic, episodic, mosaic mode of presentation.

Realism

The more 'realistic' a programme is thought to be, the more trusted, enjoyable – and therefore the more popular – it becomes. Yet realism too is an artificial construct. Its 'naturalness' arises not from nature itself but from the fact that realism is the mode in which our particular culture prefers its ritual condensations to be cast. There is nothing natural about realism, but it does correspond to the way we currently perceive the world. In this respect, it is modelled on language. We have already seen how the language we use to come to grips with the world out-there in everyday life is itself culturally constructed. Language can in fact be thought of as the *power* which allows men *to produce the natural*. Language is not, according to this definition, a 'thing' or set of objects like words, gestures, etc., it is a capacity, or competence, which can be drawn upon to produce each particular performance. (The myriad performances will in turn and over a period of time modify the competence dialectically.) In the same way realism is a competence or power which produces individual performances in the shape of realistic programmes on television like the police series or the news.

But reality is never experienced by social man in the raw. Whether the reality in question is the brute force of nature, or men's relations with other men, it is always experienced through the mediating structures of language. And this mediation is not a distortion or even a reflection of the real, it is rather the active social process through which the real is *made*. In other words, we can say that not only are signifiers (like words) arbitrary in relation to their referents, but those referents, the signifieds themselves, are equally arbitrary.

However, under normal circumstances, language does not draw much attention to its own artifice: it is in some way self-effacing. In other words, while it is the principal agency by which we create nature, it becomes at the same time 'second-nature' to us. It produces what has been termed a 'real-seemingness' where for practical purposes the *signs* for reality become the real thing. In the same way, the world of representation is made natural by the devices of realism. Those devices assume the status of second-nature by means of the thoroughly familiar conventions in which they are cast.

Television realism, then, following the pattern of language at large, 'naturalizes' the way in which we apprehend the world out-there. All the different drama series, soap operas, situation comedies, and all the news and current affairs programmes reinforce and reiterate the same connoted meaning: that the world *is*, naturally and of itself, what the mind-originated conventions of realism say it is. Realism seems to demand of us that before we can be entertained by a comedy or police drama, we must first concede that the *mode* in which the fictional story is presented is *not* constructed, but is merely the natural representation of the way things are: a *story* may be fictional, but the way it is related tells it like it is.

Certain critics have argued that realism, by projecting back into nature what amounts only to a conventional way of representing reality so that the convention and reality itself are indistinguishable, has an invidious effect on the people in the audience. It is argued that we are denied access to alternative ways of seeing, and that as a result we are obliged to accept realism's version of reality whether we like it or not. (After all, realism seems to claim, you cannot change or modify the processes of nature itself; that would be tilting at windmills.)

Hence these critics argue that realism produces in fact a 'consumerist, non-critical' attitude in the audience, whose individual member is confirmed as a mere subject, unable to influence his role. He is, in short, mystified. As we have seen in chapter 1, this argument goes on to suggest that the significance of certain artists, such as Brecht, Joyce, Sterne and Kafka, comes from their capacity to contradict the 'naturalistic fiction' of realism. They do not devote their energies to the 'production of sense' in their various messages; rather they hesitate, hold back, from the production of sense and thereby shatter, re-form and re-produce the established real-seeming. Their hesitancy defamiliarizes the conventions of their genre, putting into crisis the way in which sense passes into the realm of the natural-seeming. The effect of defamiliarization, it is suggested, is to produce in the audience or reader an awareness of the radical inadequacies of the established norms (particularly as these have established an apparent monopoly in ways of seeing) and therefore to encourage a new and critical attitude. The audience is thus rescued from its 'subjectified' consumer role, and replaced within a framework that is overtly ideo-logical and not, as is the case with realism, a framework whose ideology is hidden and self-effacing (see Ellis 1976; Barthes 1973; Parkin 1972; Lemon and Reis 1965).

This is an important argument, for, while recognizing the essential artifice of realism, it focuses our attention on the effect that the blanket coverage enjoyed by realism has on us. Is this particular blanket one which enfolds us comfort-ably, or one which smothers? Is realism capable of express-ing adequately the relationships men have established between each other and with the external world?

In the end, that question resolves itself not into *whether* realism of this kind is an adequate mode of expression, but *for whom* it is adequate. For the critics we have been discuss-ing, the answer clearly is that realism is the characteristic-ally 'bourgeois' mode of representation. To understand how this can be so, it is perhaps necessary to remind ourselves of the processes discussed towards the end of chapter 8. There we suggested that in the historical development of our class society, the dominant class's characteristic modes of thought – which we term literate modes of thought – have tended to develop along different lines from those we identify as the characteristically oral modes of thought of the subordinate class. Hence a kind of cultural lag has been produced, where-by the differing experience of the two opposing classes has resulted in fundamentally different ways of constructing reality.

Realism is a mode of representation which has its origins in literate modes of thought, and achieved its fullest expres-sion in the characteristically literate genre, the novel. Ac-cording to Watt (1957) the defining characteristics of real-ism centre on its individualism. In this respect it follows the philosophy of Descartes, whose *Meditations* 'did much to bring about the modern assumption whereby the pursuit of truth is conceived of as a wholly individual matter, logically independent of the tradition of past thought, and indeed more likely to be arrived at by a departure from it' (p. 13).

Hence in written literature from the Renaissance onwards, there can be detected 'a growing tendency for individual experience to replace collective tradition as the ultimate arbiter of reality' (p. 15). Language is radically restricted in its power of metaphoric association by realism, which produces a language 'much more largely *referential* in the novel than in other literary forms'. The novels of the earliest period set the pattern: according to Watt, the prose of Defoe and Richardson 'aims exclusively at what Locke defined as the proper purpose of language, "to convey the knowledge of things"', and their novels as a whole 'pretend to be no more than a transcription of real life' (p. 33).

The modes of thought which underlie realism can be seen as part of a more pervasive set of mind, one which has produced the characteristically bourgeois materialism of the philosophy of Descartes, and the individualism associated with Locke, whose philosophy laid the theoretical foundations for English bourgeois liberalism. For as Macpherson (1962) points out, Locke's individualism could not extend to all members of society, since it 'asserts an individuality that can only fully be realized in accumulating property, and therefore only realized by some, and only at the expense of the individuality of the others' (pp. 255–6).

Realism's claim to authenticity, its insistence on a language which functions largely as a signifier of objects – the 'knowledge of things' – together with its basic commitment to the notion of individual particularity operating within a framework claiming to be universally valid; all these characteristics set it apart as the appropriately bourgeois mode of representation. We can see that if individual experience is exalted over collective tradition, and if language is limited to the contiguity of metonym (and denied, at least in theory, the all-embracing effort of metaphoric association, resemblance and 'illogical' equivalence), then the oral tradition and collective consciousness of the subordinate class will find only an uneasy expression in the forms of realism.

Hence the suspicion voiced by the critics we discussed

earlier. A referential, authentic and individual mode which is in fact derived from the class consciousness of one class and not another will tend nevertheless to make claims on all classes. Far from being individual and particular, these claims become rather universal and timeless: realism requires that it be accepted not as *one* way of seeing but as *the* way of seeing; realism's reference is not to bourgeois modes of thought but rather to nature itself. Of course realism has been propagated far beyond the boundaries of any exclusively bourgeois audience; therefore the extent to which realism has permeated representations throughout society is a gauge of bourgeois domination within society. Seen thus, realism could be said to act as a kind of silent weapon in the extension of what amounts to bourgeois ideology over all other sections in society. The power of realism, then, resides in the appearance that its ideology *isn't there*, and that its derivation from bourgeois modes of thought is irrelevant since its version of reality is true.

The processes of history have naturalized the norms of the dominant class to an extent that realism no longer applies as a restricted technical term describing the novel. Its underlying assumptions have been imported wholesale into other modes of representation, including television.

However, realism and its underlying ideology cannot simply be *transferred* to the television medium. It must also be *transformed* by the characteristics of the medium. In television, the modes of thought which produce realism intersect with contradictory modes derived ultimately from non-literate ways of seeing. The simultaneous representation of these contradictory modes ensures that neither is excluded – though one may dominate in the form of preferred meanings. Hence there is realism and there is television realism.

Boundary rituals

It is now possible to consider how television realism's version of reality is modified by means of forms derived from a different and much more widely available tradition of cultural experience. Consider for a moment how easy it is for us, when watching the most realistic of programmes, to accept that at its beginning or end the oddest occurrences may take place. People's names appear in the sky, music emerges from nowhere, and suddenly the world we have been watching dissolves. We are unperturbed. It is easy enough to say that these manifestations are conventions to which we have become habituated, but the question remains: how is it that we accept these particular conventions so easily?

Television in fact exploits the structures we habitually use to categorize, and so make sense of, our experience of the world at large. In the case of the curious occurrences which introduce television programmes, these conform to what the anthropologist Leach calls 'boundary rituals'.

Leach (1976) shows how the boundaries between different social states – for instance the state of being single and the state of being married – are ritualized to mark the transition from one to the other. Thus being single and being married are both normal states, both are time-bound, clear-cut, central to experience and secular. But the *transition* from one to the other, the marriage ceremony, is the converse of these qualities: it is an abnormal state, it is timeless, ambiguous, at the edge of experience, sacred. Carrying the bride across the threshold powerfully signals the transition.

Whenever we cross from one category of social experience to another we tend to ritualize the transition in order to emphasize the distinction. We use signs, either verbal or non-verbal, to separate the classes or actions from each other, and thus we create artificial boundaries in a field which is in fact naturally continuous. The television message sequence is certainly naturally continuous, as witness the anxiety aroused whenever there is a break in transmission – an anxiety the broadcasters must dispel with apologies and explanations. And yet – equally naturally – the television message falls into distinct categories.

The most visible of these is the way television output is organized into discrete programmes. Hence we find that every programme has ritualized boundaries, especially at the beginning, and usually in the conventional form of the titles and credits. The distinction between different programmes is often further ritualized by what the broadcasters call *continuity*, which is the real-time reference point for the broadcasting channel, and which usually includes a look at the clock, trailers and announcements about forthcoming programmes. Continuity is easily recognized, and vital to the broadcaster and audience alike: it allows the former to transfer from one programme to the next smoothly, and the latter to adjust to the transition. Continuity also takes up a lot of television time. For instance in 1974–5 the BBC broadcast a total of 385 hours of it, representing 4·6 per cent of its output for that year, and thus comparable with the news (5·0 per cent) or drama (as opposed to light entertainment) (5·7 per cent). Music, religion, further education and schools broadcasts all trailed behind continuity in terms of hours transmitted (see the *BBC Handbook*, 1976). And yet when we watch television, continuity is treated as timeless, as a gap; it is not in any accepted sense made up of real programmes: it conforms to Leach's definition of the qualities of boundary rituals.

On commercial channels there is a different kind of boundary: that between programmes and advertisements. But it is noteworthy that this particular kind of boundary is ritualized hardly at all, signalling a perceived or desired similarity of states. Advertisements do not in themselves share the timeless, borderline characteristics of continuity – they are expected, familiar, of known duration, and so they are much more like programmes. Commercial television and our decoding of it treats advertisements and programmes as part of the *same kind* of naturally continuous field.

However, all television channels ritualize the transition from one programme to the next. We can take an example of how this is done from the British police series, *The Sweeney*, which we shall go on to discuss in more detail in the next chapter. Its boundary ritual – the title and credit sequence – is the same every week. It takes the form of a series of 'grainy' still photographs denoting a Flying Squad car (which is an unmarked saloon) approaching the camera in a succession of closer shots. A brief car chase is indicated by the same means, resulting in a still of the protagonists, Jack Regan and George Carter, holding up at gunpoint the occupants of an old Jaguar (associated with criminal getaway cars in British myths). The realistic look of the stills refers us to the codes of surveillance photography (as used by the Flying Squad). They are monochrome and convey the idea of camera-shots taken from a distance or an inconvenient location. Each photograph encapsulates a scene, and each scene builds up a sequence so that a narrative emerges. This prefigures the structure of the episode itself, as does the emphasis on sudden, unpredictable action (the Jaguar emerges from a side-road into the Squad car's path). The series' violence is prefigured in the foregrounded handguns. The close-up shots of Regan and Carter imply their prominence and interdependence. The series' excitement is ritualized by the use of cool music over the dramatic, almost stroboscopic (frozen-action) still photographs. All this activates our responses in a few seconds.

Anamnesis

The credits also slot *The Sweeney* into the paradigm of police series on television, and this is signified by the notion of a car chase culminating in a shoot-out. All the camera-shots are of the streets, signifying an anonymous location, and yet the individual heroes are foregrounded for identification – in contrast to the villains. (The similar minor credits at the end of each programme do show Regan and Carter in an institutional setting, signified by phones, and interior shots of the office.) Hence the opening credits are not only a boundary ritual, they are also 'anamnesic' – they perform the function of 'bringing to mind' what the audience already knows about *The Sweeney* in particular, and the paradigm of the police series in general. In fact a boundary ritual must not be thought of as separating discrete programmes so much as connecting them.

Indeed, the function of anamnesis is encoded formally into the boundary rituals of many realistic series. Some, like *Starsky and Hutch*, *Charlie's Angels* and *Play for Today*, use either stills or clips from previous episodes of the same series: we are reminded of what we may well already have seen, and it is thereby suggested that what we are about to receive will make us similarly satisfied. Other series, such as *The Rockford Files* and *Police Woman*, encode clips of the action which is about to take place in the particular episode: here we are being reminded that what we have not yet seen is part of a paradigm to which we are accustomed and which we find entertaining. Certain advertisements employ the same kind of anamnesic connection.

The anamnesic function works not merely by reminding us of a familiar paradigm, but equally by switching off, as it were, our capacity to read it in terms of another paradigm. But, as Leach (1976) points out, meanings *depend* upon contrast. The different programmes which together make up television's total-output paradigm mean what they do in opposition to each other. Just as red and green lights only mean stop and go when opposed to each other in a particular context on the highway, so *The Sweeney* means what it does because it is not, for instance, the *News at Ten* – it can be contrasted with the news for its identity to emerge.

Let us consider the boundary ritual of the *News at Ten*, which is generally the programme immediately following *The Sweeney*, after advertisements and continuity. The chief sign used in the title sequence of *News at Ten* is a photograph of Big Ben, showing ten o'clock. The photograph of the clock (iconic, motivated sign) is a *metonym* for the building as a whole. The building (the Houses of Parliament) is a *metonym* for the institution of government which is centred in it, and indeed it is difficult for us to disentangle the metonymy of the name 'House of Commons' sufficiently to distinguish the building from the activity that takes place inside and around it. However, that activity (government) is a *metaphor* for public life in general, and hence the single iconic sign of Big Ben telescopes into itself the meaning that the *News at Ten* is about public life in general.

Journalistic codes are simultaneously present in the same sign, so that the fact that the clock shows ten o'clock which is (normally) the real time at which the news is broadcast, refers us to the journalistic myths of urgency, immediacy, of an up-to-the-minute report on the world. Film/television codes, in the form of the increasingly urgent music as the camera pans across the London skyline before zooming dramatically into Big Ben's clockface, reinforce this meaning of the sign. Not only do we see the clock, we also hear its chimes – between each of which one main headline is read. However, we certainly don't hear all ten, usually four or five, and if we were to time the intervals between each chime we would discover that there is often a half-second's or second's irregularity. In fact the chimes are produced in the studio at the touch of a button, and each one is timed to fit the headline it follows. In other words, they are a kind of aural metonomy, and we are invited to see and hear through them the real Big Ben striking real time. Pre-television codes (our everyday experience) predispose us to believe that what we see on the screen is actually happening. The broadcasters rely on this habit of thought, using it successfully to *create* the real.

Once the 'real' is established as such, it becomes a vehicle for the communication of messages which embody, not our 'real' social relationships, but rather cultural mythologies *about* these relationships. It only remains to consider, then, the mythological uses to which television's artificial reality is put.

12 A POLICEMAN'S LOT

A Man Called Ironside is a conscious enactment of the values of an ordered, stable, liberal-conservative society. Its very existence as such presupposes that such values are on the defensive, and as a result it may appear to be of a piece with some of the products of the 'nostalgia boom' of the early 1970s. However, these products, such as *Upstairs Downstairs*, *Colditz*, *Edward VII*, *The Forsyte Saga* and other dramatized novels, are all set in the past. *Ironside* has to relate its nostalgia-based values much more explicitly to the contemporary city.

A fair cop

A clear example of the *Ironside* mode is to be found in an episode called *The Last Cotillion*, screened in the autumn of 1976. Its heroine, Athena Champion, is bound to the past by a guilty secret. The function of the investigation is to uncover this secret, bring the guilty to justice, and offer ritual forgiveness and thus an adjustment which enables the heroine to free herself from the bounds of the past and move into a contemporary life.

The early scenes of the episode serve to establish the upper-class milieu within which the drama unfolds, showing in addition that Ironside himself is thoroughly at home among such company. He is asked by Athena on the basis of their friendship to investigate two murders, which she suspects have been committed by herself. There is overwhelming 'evidence' given to persuade the viewer that this is indeed the case: she has been sleepwalking, she appears to have a motive, and the ritualized slow-motion shots of the murders themselves show the viewer a face that is 'clearly' hers. But Ironside is not convinced. He uses his intellect and the technological resources of the police department to piece together a story which goes back to the golden age of Athena's youth, and thereby discovers her secret. As his investigation proceeds, the viewer is given corroborating evidence, so that there is a transformation of our view of what it is that the facts 'say'. The secret which binds Athena to the past is a graphic and simple one – she has a twin sister, who is kept in a secret apartment at the top of the Champion mansion. She has lost her reason, and is thought by all outsiders to have died after giving birth to a daughter many years before. It emerges that she is activated by that daughter to commit the murders and thus to throw suspicion on Athena. Of course, the daughter has appeared hitherto to be one of Athena's few supporters – a stance which is revealed to have been the means by which she leads Athena deeper into the desired self-destruction. The audience is further deceived by being lead to suspect the mad woman's husband and apparent widower, Courtney Elliott, who is the black sheep of the family. His seemingly upright daughter confirms our suspicions by refusing to have anything to do with him.

In the first scene of the fable, we are introduced to Athena's luxurious and old-fashioned living room. But modernity is already here, in the guise of Courtney Elliott, whose very name signifies upper-class Anglo-Saxon decadence to an American viewer. He helps himself to a drink and thus deliberately breaks the code of courtesy by which Athena lives. She tells him he is *persona non grata* in the house, to which he replies: 'My dear sister-in-law, there's never been any doubt in my mind that I'm unwelcome here' – again stressing that his value system and hers are in conflict. When, nevertheless, he is asked his business he replies:

Elliott: It, Athena dear, is the rising cost of living. Of course I realize you are sheltered from such mundane considerations, but unfortunately I'm not so lucky. You would be shocked at the cost of food, of Napoleon Brandy, and these handsome shirts McAlia's makes especially for me. I hate to tell you, Athena old girl, but you're just going to have to make an 'adjustment' in our 'arrangement'.

Athena: Why don't you call it by its proper name?

Elliott: It doesn't matter what we call it. It will have to be doubled.

Courtney Elliott can be signified to us by simple metonymic signs in the confidence that we will perform the role demanded of us by metonymy – that of finding and responding to the whole of which the sign refers us to a part. The ease with which we achieve this indicates how centrally that 'whole' concerns us. Courtney Elliott is not established as a 'character' in any way, but as a 'functional sign' – part of the function of bringing the old into conflict with the new. This same function is performed by another middle-aged character of the same circle as Elliott, one Tony. He has flirtatiously proposed to Athena, pressing her to abandon the Champion mansion and come to live with him – married or not. She laughs at this 'modern' notion at the outset of the episode, but at the end her role in the resolution of the tensions is signified by her acceptance of a cruise in Tony's company – where it is emphasized that they are to share a cabin without having married. Thus Athena enters the modern world.

Elliott and Tony are the only two men in Athena's world

to survive in the episode, and they show simply and graphically that there are good and bad, acceptable and unacceptable ways of adapting to the new. It is significant too that Elliott is bad only because of the *way* in which he applies his materialist, pragmatic values, not because he actually holds them. His fate is not to receive approbation, it is merely to survive. This distinguishes him from his daughter who is motivated by hatred and jealousy, and is characterized by her dissembling and nearly fatal 'loyalty' to Athena's values. She is bad, and thus she and what she stands for is rejected – appropriately we see her being led away by the police for just retribution.

The viewer is expected to sympathize with the conservative value system portrayed, to find in its formality, courtesy and stability a recompense for the loss of such values in our daily social experience. Yet at the same time the viewer is continually reminded that this value system is doomed; he is being asked to sympathize with the loser, and thus to recognize that his own conservative value system needs updating, however distasteful this might appear. Indeed, this episode of *Ironside* is a means of ritually structuring the conflicts felt by such viewers: once the old values have been placed under stress, it is presumably reassuring to discover that the protagonists can emerge cheerfully into the 'new world'. *Ironside* presents a model of the *need* to adapt, and it also presents metonymic signs by which the viewer can grasp the *means* to adapt.

The ideology of intervention

But there are two microcosms portrayed in this episode. One is the outdated conservative world of Athena Champion, and the other is the contemporary conservative world of Ironside and his team. Ironside invites the viewer to accept him as a spokesman, and his investigations enact the bard at work, explaining and evaluating the moral constructs of whichever world he enters each week, and providing the means by which the eternal conflicts in those worlds can be resolved.

Ironside himself is naturally full of significance. His wheelchair serves not only to identify him, but, more importantly, is an overt sign that he uses non-physical and non-violent methods. Here he resembles Cannon, who is 'disabled' by his fat belly, which he constantly foregrounds. Cannon's disability is not as severe as Ironside's, so he is often attacked although he never initiates violence. Another 'disabled' detective is Harry O, who is not legless but carless. Ironside embodies a common-sense kind of intellectualism, which manifests itself as clear-headedness and knowledge of people. He cannot himself be the victim of physical violence, since attacking the disabled is taboo in our culture. Hence *Ironside* lacks the appeal of the kind of action sequence associated with series like *Starsky and Hutch*.

Ironside's appeal lies in other directions. The world he moves in, for instance, embodies his values. He is a respected and senior man with maximum individual freedom of action, and yet at the same time he is able to tap the resources of a modern and technological institution. He is free from the constraints of paperwork, of having to define his activities in institutional terms, but still he gains much of his power from his institutional status. His team is self-contained and independent. Hence he is a free agent, self-motivating and self-disciplined; an entrepreneur and western individualist in harmony with modern complex institutions. His office is a further sign of this status. It is a cross between an office and an apartment, furnished in wood and in an ample, Edwardian style. His work is also his life, but it is not the pen-pushing of the glass and steel office, it is the contemplation of the scholar. He is, incidentally, clearly free of any material wants.

His team comprises Ed, the young, white male – he is an extension of Ironside into the physical dimension, to be used when violence, footwork or routine paperwork is necessary. Then there is Mark the black, who is Ironside's driver. His blackness is in a sense incidental to his *job* in the series (which could be performed by anyone) but of course his *function* is to show a black integrated into Ironside's social microcosm. Thus he represents a defused racial relationship. The same applies to Fran, the woman. Her presence in the 'male' world of law enforcement is foregrounded, her function being to complement the blackness of Mark and the youth of Ed. But her function too is belied by her job, which is often to spot 'feminine' clues (as in this episode, where orchid flowers are significant) or to perform feminine (drudge) tasks.

Ironside's team is presented as a harmonious society – part hunting party out of American mythology, part microcosm of western class structures. But in terms of the way this 'society' is presented in the series itself, Ironside's team derive their satisfying meaning not only from their metonymic reference but also by binary opposition to each other:

    male : female
    white : black
    cerebral : physical
    age : youth

The left-hand set of terms show the 'esteemed' or dominant values of this series. It is interesting to notice how the integration of these values into a harmonious society is presented as natural, and this offers us a graphic example of what Barthes terms the 'ex-nominating' process that operates in the ideology of our society. The structure of these relationships is never foregrounded for inspection or criticism, but appears as the natural order, and as such does not require any conscious statement – it does not need to be *named* (Barthes 1973, pp. 138–41). Hence any contradictions in this structure, as for instance between the subordinate characters' function (to relate to each other and to Ironside as a harmonious society) and their jobs (to do menial, unpleasant or delegated tasks), are simply never shown as contradictions. Only an aberrant decoding by the audience will bring them out, if the audience's view of social relations does not fit that of the series.

All *Ironside* episodes are homologues of each other – their structure is the same. The third-order mythologies are re-iterated each week. We are constantly reminded that individual freedom of action is esteemed, that stable but unstated moral codes underpin social relationships, and that an individual can, despite apparent disabilities (like a wheel-chair) control, explain, and adapt to his environment. In this respect there is a notable resemblance between Ironside (fiction) and Bill Graham, the shepherd, in our *News at Ten* bulletin (fact). It may be that Ironside's success as an individual depends upon the willing (and unconscious) collaboration of his team, but this is presented not so much as part of the environment to which Ironside must adapt, but rather as an extension of himself on which he can depend.

The only changes from week to week are in the iconic signifiers of these mythologies, and in particular the various signifiers (often called characters) for the problems Ironside must solve. *Ironside* as a series is in fact differentiated from some others in the police series genre by its self-assured superiority over the world Ironside puts to rights. He is paternalist, in the sense that he intervenes, usually unasked, into the lives of people who cannot compete with him simply because we see them for one episode only: their function is to be the embodiment of problems upon which Ironside can bring his ideology to bear. The effect is, first, to make all who move into Ironside's world dependent upon him, and second, to test the efficacy of his ideology. Its content is obviously never open to question. Apart from express-ing formulaic 'truths' or the story's moral, he never needs to expound the ideology as such. All that is required is that it should be seen to prevail over the problem.

The language of violence

Despite the powerful formula by which *Ironside* works, the series as a whole is under stress, suffering from the competition of other series which are currently more socio-central than *Ironside* has become. These include a succession of American series from *Kojak* through *Starsky and Hutch* to *Bionic Woman* and *Charlie's Angels*, and such British productions as Thames Television's *The Sweeney*. We propose now to consider *The Sweeney* in more detail.

'Programmes such as *The Quest, Starsky and Hutch* on BBC and *The Sweeney* on ITV, have on some days made the hour between 9 p.m. and 10 p.m. one of the most violent on British television.' This judgement was delivered in the recent Annan Report on *The Future of Broadcasting* (1977, p. 253). The Report was commissioned by the government to enable it to decide how to organize broadcasting into the 1990s, and was the largest official enquiry into British broadcasting ever undertaken. Its judgement represents not only the reputation of *The Sweeney* itself, but also what Annan calls 'the glorification of violence' on television in general (p. 260).

That so august a body should feel impelled to make weighty comments on television entertainment demonstrates clearly how deep is the fear of the power of television. But its comments on television violence, though carefully considered, share with many less well-read criticisms a fundamental misapprehension about what television violence actually involves. Simply, the Annan Report raises to the level of official policy the confusion of *enacted* violence, or *images* of violence, with violence itself. The distinction is more important than may at first appear.

The Annan Report took account of a large body of research into television violence, and concluded, 'the results are clear; violence is frequent' (p. 249). But as shown in chapter 2, head-counting – even the counting of rolled heads – is not enough. Violence on television is not 'displayed' (as the Annan Report puts it) as if through a window; it is in fact a semiotic category. It is a vehicle through which meanings are transferred: one technically suited to the television medium with visual, active face-to-face (or fist-to-face) contact that fills the optimum mid-shot/close-up range of the television camera frame. As we have noted, violence normally occurs between two people, at close range – but the people in question are more often than not strangers to each other. Violence between intimates (husband/wife, for instance) is rare and would tend to shock (that is, to break the convention). Hence violence on television is more common than it is in real life for the same kind of reasons that prestige occupations are more common on television than they are in real life: both are symbolic representations of social values. Violence enacts social, rather than personal relations; it takes place between personalized moralities (good *v.* bad, efficient *v.* inefficient, culturally esteemed *v.* culturally deviant) rather than between individual people *per se*. There is perhaps no more economical and visually arresting way of enacting social conflicts which are in essence abstract and located in the mind than by means of an enacted slugging match (if there was, no doubt the television producers would have found and used it). Further, the audience is so habituated to these conventional modes of behaviour that there is little risk of their mistaking television violence for anything other than conventional behaviour. It is not easy to imitate in one's individual physical form the ritualized conflict between abstract ideas and moralities. Just as Elizabethan London failed to dissolve into carnage and parricide after the audience of *Hamlet* spilled out of the theatre, so modern Londoners desist from mass brutality after an episode of *The Sweeney*. On television, violence is only, after all, the continuation of language by other means.

Indeed, television violence can be thought of as essentially conservative in its effect rather than destructive. This is because it is difficult to avoid resolving a fist fight or a shoot-out: the conflict is resolved one way or the other, usually of course in favour of the socially esteemed morality. Often one or two esteemed but expendable *personae* (such as women) are done away with before the ultimately inefficient villain gets what's coming to him in the last scene. But this merely enlarges his threat and therefore puffs up the satisfaction that is felt as he drops groaning out of camera-shot (and out of our memories). Television violence too often disposes of really intractable sources of social tension, dislocation or conflict with a neat, bloodless hole in the villain's heart.

But it is possible that in some programmes the violence may emerge as something of a character in its own right. One such programme is *The Sweeney*. There are occasions in this series when the choreography of the fights evokes rather more anxiety for the safety of the actors than conventional fights do. Tighter close-ups are used; clubs are wielded (never aimed at the head but always at the body, and the recipient crumples like a ragdoll); faces are distorted by stocking-masks; large numbers of people are involved (the Squad *v.* the Gang); participants are observed looking hurt and even bloody (in one episode both the main characters sported black eyes for the remaining half of the story after a fight); and finally, editing is organized to exploit the maximum surprise in cuts. As a result, the violence of *The Sweeney* lingers on in the mind of the viewer. It is still a ritual condensation of social conflicts, still a means of communication between the centre and the deviant, but it often seems more prolonged than is conventionally necessary. It draws attention to itself, becomes defamiliarized and so introduces a new element into the drama. The effect is one that takes account of the growing dissatisfaction on the part of the audience with the neat, bloodless hole. That particular convention has become a cliché, and *The Sweeney* responds by saying in its prolonged and nasty fights that the old answers will not serve, that problems and conflicts can still be solved, but at greater risk, with greater suffering, and with less confidence in the outcome. *The Sweeney*'s type of violence is defensive, reactive, and speaks to an audience whose own comfortable assumptions about affluence, security, personal prestige and power have suffered attrition ever since the 1960s.

Paradigmatic contrasts

Clearly, then, *The Sweeney* is telling us not only what it is, but at the same time what it is not. Speaking in the codes and acting in the conventions of the police series, *The Sweeney* sets itself apart from those that are rooted in older and more self-confident traditions: series such as *Ironside*. Its reaction against the codes of *Ironside* is not confined merely to the paradigm of violence.

In *Ironside* there is a sense of unremitting domesticity, signified by the concentration of internal shots, dialogue and lack of physical action. Ironside's politeness, courtesy and method of investigation demand such a setting, and the use of family groups as the source of many of his investigations produces an ambience of paternal intervention into the (childlike) problems of people, often young/female, who cannot look after themselves and for whom Ironside represents (on behalf of the viewer) a protective security. *The Sweeney*'s setting is such that 'domestic' takes on a different connotation. Homes are where wives are interviewed alone, often with sexual undertones implied between them and the police; and homes are alien to the Squad – they do not intervene, they invade. Homes are also the setting for the operations of the villains, which results in their devaluation since they become targets rather than refuges. In an episode called *Selected Target*, screened in September 1976, domesticity is not only violated, it becomes a positive liability: an innocent banker is recruited by the villains to perform a complex fraud as a result of his wife and child being held hostage in their own home.

Again, Ironside's interventionist stance is avoided in *The Sweeney*. Here the police do not perform a role of conflict resolution, they initiate conflict as a way of precipitating action. And action is directed towards the next step in a continuing game of skill, whereby they predict the moves of the villains, often with the aid of sophisticated technological surveillance techniques. They test their skill against the circumstances supplied by fate or the villains themselves. Hence it is not so necessary in *The Sweeney* for the police to win every case – one of the conventions established in the *Ironside*-type series deliberately broken here is that of the infallibility of the good guys.

Starsky and Hutch is exactly contemporary with *The Sweeney* in terms of peak popularity. Like *The Sweeney*, it presents a paradigmatic contrast with *Ironside*, but, as we shall see, only as far as the second order. Thus, where Ironside is middle-aged, Starsky and Hutch are youthful; where he is immobile they are highly mobile; where he is cerebral they are physical; where he is an individual they are a team; where he is suburban they are urban, etc. Hence *Starsky and Hutch* triggers different myths from those of *Ironside* to the extent that the iconic images of the two derive from a different cultural experience. Indeed, one of the messages propagated most systematically by *Starsky and Hutch* is that it is not a police series at all. The protagonists' dress is paradigmatically contrasted with police dress; their car is in contrast with police cars; their behaviour and relationship with each other is contrasted with expected police behaviour. This may well be in response to the bad image of the American police in recent years, especially among people younger than middle-aged. Conversely, *Ironside* is much more police-oriented and possibly for the same reason – that it upholds the traditional image of the police in the face of iconoclastic social pressures.

However, where the very different first- and second-order signs of *Ironside* and *Starsky and Hutch* respectively cohere into mythologies, a much greater congruence can be observed. Like Ironside, Starsky and Hutch are interventionists. They are remote from the criminals they pursue, and are highly differentiated from them. Indeed, an important character in the series is their informant and link with the criminal world, Huggy Bear. He is a 'black' black – in opposition to Starsky and Hutch's superior, the police captain, who is a 'white' black. Huggy Bear is uncompromisingly black in looks and behaviour; and as such he represents visually a socially 'deviant' subgroup. On the other hand, his character is entertaining and he maintains a jolly friendship with Starsky and Hutch, hence his role as a channel of communication between them and the criminal world. They cannot communicate directly on equal terms with the criminal (socially deviant) world, largely because they are identifiable as 'good' only to the extent that they are opposed to the criminals who are 'bad'. Like Ironside, Starsky and Hutch keep their distance from, and act *on* their world, imposing their own structure, which syntagmatically is close to Ironside's, on the weekly succession of data. The world as posited by these two iconically dissimilar programmes, then, is largely the same world at the ideological level.

Displacement

But *The Sweeney* provides a further contrast within the police series format, and in fact represents a different relationship with the world out-there from that of the two American series. The title of *The Sweeney* focuses the difference. The title is that of the institution, not the individual foregrounded in it. And yet the institution is not defined according to its own view of itself. The Sweeney is the name given to the Flying Squad by its adversaries: in cockney rhyming slang Flying Squad = Sweeney Todd; hence The Sweeney. Here, a systematic and specifically located violence is done to language. Rhyming slang in fact *displaces* ordinary language, showing us a world where the institution (the police) speaks the same language as its clients (the criminals) so that there is a levelling effect between the two. It brings to our mind an awareness of the more fundamental displacement which we discussed earlier in terms of

violence on television: the concerns, relationships and conflicts which propel the sequence of pre-television reality
(everyday life) are displaced into a narrative sequence.

Regan and Carter employ 'deviant' methods in their
detection, just as Starsky and Hutch do. But in *The Sweeney*
there is less evidence of an artificial distinction between the
cops' deviant behaviour and that of the criminals. Indeed,
in the episode called *Selected Target*, Inspector Regan is
shown rifling his superior's office in an attempt to find what
has been said about him in the supposedly confidential
annual report. This criminal behaviour is shown as quite
normal and while he is doing it he discusses with Sergeant
Carter the details of the latest case. Eventually Carter puts
Regan out of his misery by quoting from the report at
length – he too has used his legitimate detection powers to
find the report: in the typing pool. Significantly, the institution's view of Regan in the report dwells on his anti-
authoritarian attitudes. Again, in many episodes both
Regan and Carter are involved in brutal fist fights. This
behaviour is legitimated in television codes, but in *The
Sweeney* it acquires new meanings when we see Carter being
set upon by a gang of heavies, who, after beating him up,
are revealed to be policemen from another squad – they
have mistaken Carter for a criminal just as we mistake them.
By these means the congruence of the deviant and legitimate
worlds is enacted.

But the function of anamnesis (bringing to mind) does not
require a conscious or systematic awareness of the way in
which *The Sweeney*'s metaphorical relationship with reality
works (and indeed the common misapprehension about the
difference between TV violence and actual violence suggests that the awareness is far from conscious). More
important for the viewer of *The Sweeney* is that it should be
relevant, meaningful and entertaining – that is, that its
mythology should emerge, exploiting the characteristics of the
medium and of the narrative, even while the viewer might
consciously be worrying about the effect of the violence, the

non-legitimate behaviour of the heroes, or other apparently deviant denotations.

In fact, the third-order mythology of *The Sweeney* is much less a matter of individual free agents imposing a particular world-view on given events than is the case in *Starsky and Hutch* or *Ironside*. *The Sweeney*'s world is defensive; events are unpredictable, and although the cops and robbers know each other very well, neither group at the denotative order fits in with the rest of society. In another sequence from *Selected Target* we can see how this is achieved. A known villain, Colley Kibber, is under surveillance, suspected of planning a big crime. He knows who is watching him and how to react. He imports two call girls, and has them undress for him. This is an accepted sign of 'unsuspecting behaviour' in his code, and the policemen with cameras secreted in the block of flats opposite begin to relax and enjoy the show. We too are drawn into the deception as viewers, since the offer of the unusually frank visual images of the girls, shown in the form of police surveillance stills, is used to lull us as well as the police. While all attention is riveted on the scene behind the 'casually' open curtains, a gang of heavies is able to slip unnoticed into the block of flats and burst in on the photographers. They know immediately what is expected of them, and a fight begins. This spills over into one of the flats, where the occupants are seated around the meal table watching television. Their world is exploded amid shrieks and smashed furniture, as the fight casually spills back into the corridor. A baby's pram becomes a weapon when a villain falls on to it and is catapulted feet first into a wall by three of the policemen. Meanwhile Kibber has produced the desired effect – all the surrounding police are drawn to the scene of the fight, and he slips away. We are here so involved in the highly skilled game played by the police and criminals that when images of family life, prams, homes, which under other circumstances would signify security and like-usness are violated with so little concern, we are not encouraged to object. For however deviant *The Sweeney*'s action is at the denotative order, its mythology of defensive determination to cope in insecure and hostile circumstances is peculiarly appropriate for a society in a period of recession.

The television of recession

The Sweeney's world is not one where 'white hat' restores the accepted moralities by the mere act of shooting 'black hat'. Their world is unpredictable, episodic, present-tense. They react to events rather than manipulating them – just as British frigates react to Icelandic gunboats and the British army to the IRA. Their domestic life is not the stable scholastic comfort which Ironside enjoys. When off duty (or even when on duty) *The Sweeney*'s male is either marking time, drinking, or attempting to pull a bird – often in competition with one of his colleagues. On the rare occasions when Regan is shown at home he does not sit, he stands. The home is merely another location where he can keep in contact with the real world of the streets – the foregrounded feature is the phone, together with the beer-stocked fridge and the electric kettle. His home-life is not stressed, but sketchy details are given. These enrich the series' unglamorous verisimilitude by hinting at domestic troubles to match Regan's professional ones. The overall mythology which emerges is one where perceptions of social permanency are constantly challenged, but where a man with internal motivation and skill can carve out an acceptable set of personal relations and professional achievements. Hostility is expected from and shown to both the higher reaches of the authoritarian institution and the external world.

The relations between individuals and their institutions is in fact one of *The Sweeney*'s most complex elements. The villains, for example, are rarely if ever individuals acting alone – usually they are surrounded by accountants, lawyers and women as well as the usual henchmen. This increases their legitimacy as targets in a world where bourgeois security is regarded with a jaundiced eye. The deviant 'aping' of legitimate business enterprise confers the impersonal powers of the business institution on the villains, who act not only as criminals but as criminal bosses. This enables the audience to identify more easily with Regan and Carter in a society where the overwhelming majority of the people have no share in the ownership and control of the institutions they work for.

But the focus of attention is Regan's relationship with Carter. It is not the same kind of relationship as that between Starsky and Hutch. The latter is one of equality – their rank in the police force is the same. They are more boyish; there are fraternity-based codes underlying much of their dialogue, which is, however, less important than their non-verbal behaviour: they exchange meaningful looks (which not only cement their friendship but set them apart from the characters who are excluded from the looks), there is much body contact, signalling an unselfconscious affection, and their stance is relaxed. Their cognitive processes are basically the same – 'are you thinking what I'm thinking?' The American myth of a social dissonance between college graduates and non-college men is introduced as a potential tension to their relationship, but only one to be overcome. For instance, when both are trapped in a building which is airtight, college-boy Hutch starts using maths to compute how long they can survive while practical Starsky starts looking around the given setting for a means to escape. The manual non-college man, who is the team's driver and Jewish, just as Ironside's driver and action-man is black, is married to his more intellectual counterpart in a fruitful relationship which works because it transcends the dissonance: their differing methods make the team as a whole more efficient.

Carter, however, is not Regan's equal, he is his sergeant. Their relationship is one of fruitful friendship too, and they compete equally with each other for women, jokes and theories about the current case. Carter has even been shown competing for Regan's status by trying for the rank of inspector. In personal terms there is no distinction between the two. But in professional terms there is. The camera is 'focused' on Regan and while he is constrained in his freedom of action only by the police hierarchy, Carter is constrained by his own identity, which is defined in subordination to Regan. Hence Regan can be anti-authoritarian, since that suggests a stance towards an external social pressure. Carter shares this stance, but he cannot be anti-authoritarian in the same way, since his superior authority is Regan. Regan relies on Carter to back him up, and uses both Carter and his own anti-authoritarian stance as positive and helpful means by which he creates his personal living space. *The Sweeney* tells us that in a period when 'real life' offers us wage-restraint, inflation and a fall in living standards, there is no need for class hostility. The Regan/Carter relationship personalizes for the television audience a point of view which places two 'classes' in a hostile environment and shows how working together can produce individual satisfaction for both – though *not* equality for the subordinate 'class'. Hence *The Sweeney* presents a society where class divisions are overcome because both 'classes' – Regan and Carter – share the same outlook on life, methods and language. They do not share the same status, but are presented as finding no tension in this position. Carter is presented as being fully satisfied in his subordination, a subordination that is acceptable because of the personal value discerned in Regan (whose language and behaviour codes are themselves working-class in mode). Thus *The Sweeney* shares with *Starsky and Hutch* and *Ironside* the 'personalization' of status relationships, in much the same way as the other version of reality – news reporting – personalizes the social forces which produce the events reported.

CONCLUSION: SOMETHING COMPLETELY DIFFERENT?

BROADCAST news and the police series have much in common. If the police series is a metaphoric displacement of the events of real life, then television news is a metonym of the same events. Both, however, tend to establish syntagmatic structures which allow the viewer to recognize and distinguish the particular show he is watching from week to week or day to day. The news operates with a limited number of known elite people, who recur over many episodes, and are largely drawn from the world of politics. The way they are presented depends upon their cultural function rather than whatever they might be doing.

This cast of familiar people together with their equally familiar setting of economics, politics, foreign affairs and so on provides a syntagmatic structuring into which the paradigmatic unpredictable events of each day are slotted and so given meaning. News reporting's other great preoccupation, with disasters, accidents and human interest stories, provides a parallel syntagm whereby man's relationship with the world out-there is structured. Like *The Sweeney* and *Starsky and Hutch*, news reporting progresses by means of short scenes which superficially present unconnected material. A wide variety of signifiers using a variety of modes, from different newsreaders to film, graphics and stills, is used to present a very limited number of signifieds:

the signs in both cases cohere into mythological sets whose content is reiterated over and over again.

But in the presentation of news there is a greater intervention than in police series of the pre-televisual codes of literacy. That is, clarity, consistency, 'logical' exposition of causes, balance, precision; all are derived via journalistic codes from the modes of thought appropriate to literate discourse. Many of the criticisms levelled at news reporting on television are based on a belief that these are the very codes to which such reporting fails to adhere. It is widely held that 'triviality', 'sensationalism', and the habit of presenting a story for its visual impact rather than for its 'importance' demonstrate 'falling standards'. A good example of this view is to be found in the writings of Robin Day, who is himself a highly respected political commentator in British television. He criticizes the current half-hour television news programmes for being

> a tabloid kaleidoscope of events – the televisual version of a newspaper's front page headlines, with only a fraction of the story content. Though the main facts are covered, their news value is liable to be affected by an overemphasis on what is available by way of direct visual coverage of events. This tends to be edited so as to select the most visibly emotive or violent part for transmission ... It is quite common that a television news item has given the bare facts, but is so short on explanation as to make it little more than a signal to find out what it means in tomorrow morning's newspapers. (1975, p. 62)

Television's chief failing, in other words, is that it is television. Indeed, Day's suggestion to the Annan Committee for an improved television news service was to propose what he calls, revealingly, a 'newspaper of the screen'. However, his view that television news acts merely as a signal that has to be interpreted by another subsequent set of signals in the preferred literate mode not only ignores television's own strengths as a medium, but also overstates the supposed advantages of the print media over it. For example, for those (millions) of the population who are tuned into the bulletin, the news means all the news: it is far less easy to avoid an item in an unbroken sequence than it is to skip a page or two of a newspaper. As for having only a 'fraction of the story content' of a front page headline, the opening item in our *News at Ten* bulletin lasted approximately six minutes, covered the story from six different angles, contained over 1450 words, and showed three different newsfilms. It was in fact a fuller account of the events in Northern Ireland than appeared in any newspaper the following day with the possible exception of *The Daily Telegraph* (which nevertheless only covered the same points). Of course, there is a kind of *intertextuality* between television news and newspapers which means that, because the two media are appealing to broadly the same people, the popular newspapers at least have abandoned some of their news-carrying function to television. Conversely, television itself often makes good news-copy in the papers. In other words, the two media are interdependent and complementary.

But the most significant aspect of Robin Day's criticism is that it is his. He writes as an experienced and well-known practitioner of the serious political business of television. The fact that he is reduced to voicing his criticisms in print, while being constrained to continue working within the conditions he dislikes, is a measure of the inability of literate elite opinion to manipulate television into the form that best suits literate definitions of the situation. Robin Day represents within himself one of television's most important 'active contradictions'.

The contradictions inherent in television's handling of reality go further than the news. For instance, most sport presented on television is now mediated by a full apparatus of commentators, studios full of experts, charts, potted histories and above all discussion – a format not dissimilar to that used for political elections. By these means the television version of sport imposes a literacy on games such as football which is not experienced by the fans on the terraces, whose view of it tends to be collective, locality-based and class-conscious. On television, football is invested with other values: games become part of a narrative sequence; physicality is played down; the referee is always right (as the representative of externally defined authority); and goals – achievement of the competitive 'goal' – are subject to idolatry. Hence there is sport and there is television sport. Television sport is experienced by a different section of the population, certainly a wider one, from those who experience live sport. But the active contradictions structured into this mediation are always present in the television presentation, and can surface embarrassingly for the unwary commentator.

Contradictions of a different kind surface in the kind of police series we have discussed at length. For a good example, take the series *Bionic Woman*. This series shows a woman in social roles traditionally reserved to men. Jaime Sommers is strong, able to fight and beat men. She upholds those moral values which she asserts with her bionic right arm, and defends us from the plots she identifies with her bionic ear. In all this she represents a willingness on behalf of our society to see women as men's equals. But of course society itself has not yet translated the willingness into fact, and neither has Jaime Sommers. Despite her manly role she is still a man's view of a woman: polite, willing to make her boss's coffee, and attractively dressed according to male definitions of attractiveness. In fact, although this series is focused on a woman, its male chauvinism is more pronounced than that of a series like *The Sweeney*, despite that series' masculine aggressiveness. As Buscombe (1976) notes, *The Sweeney* displays 'the undisguised chauvinism of the working class as opposed to the subtler chauvinism of the middle class' (p. 67). As a result, perhaps, women in *The Sweeney* are often able to trade their role as sex-objects for power in the game of survival. They are thereby able to create sufficient 'defensible space' for themselves to achieve a measure of autonomy. Jaime Sommers, on the other hand, is fully incorporated into male definitions, and is frequently obliged to disguise her male-bionic strength to avoid embarrassing a weaker male. She also uses her powers for the most traditional of female tasks – an episode called *Mirror Image*, screened in 1977, had her doing bionic housework in a supposedly lighthearted sequence quite irrelevant to the plot.

Interestingly, several episodes of *Bionic Woman* have used the idea of mistaken identity – in *Mirror Image* she is captured and replaced by a look-alike who attempts to steal information 'vital to national security' which if lost could 'jeopardize the SALT talks'. The manifest intention is to spin a traditional spy yarn out of the programme's formula which places women in high places – but the choice of the particular vehicle of mistaken identity is revealing. It seems to signify a social unease with the identity of women in such roles. Women suffer the lack of traditional and unspoken male ties (such as old school ties) upon which trust can be placed. Jaime Sommers is one of us, certainly, but how do we know it's Jaime Sommers?

Conventional television, which most members of the audience are content to take as they find, is thus unable to answer the great questions of our time. But equally it is unable to avoid (albeit tacitly and in the form of contradictions) asking those same questions. The answers are left to the audience, whose freedom to decode as they collectively choose is built in to the medium's structure, and built in in such a way that it is influenced more by the collective meaning systems of the culture at large than by any explicit manipulation on the part of the producers.

Throughout this book we have insisted on the extent to which television is dependent upon more general cultural processes for its messages, modes and meanings. It might seem, as a result of this stance, that we are putting forward the case that television is 'only obeying orders', and that therefore you must take it or leave it. In fact we imply the reverse. Semiotics is beginning to reveal to us the extent to which our universe is 'man-made', and we have argued in this chapter, as in the rest of the book, that 'reality' on television is a human construction. Furthermore, it is a construction which can be analysed.

Developing an awareness of how a particular reality is produced can enable us to avoid misconceptions about the nature of that reality. In addition, it can lead to constructive criticism. As Eco (1972) has put it:

> In political activity it is not indispensable to change a given message: it would be enough (or perhaps better) to change the attitude of the audience, so as to induce a different decoding of the message – or in order to isolate the intentions of the transmitter and thus to criticize them. (p. 121)

Critical analysis of this kind can of course take several forms. On the one hand we can observe the growth in educational institutions of both research and courses, part of the purpose of which is precisely to subject the television message to systematic criticism. On the other hand, it is noticeable that the medium itself is developing the kind of self-confidence that can admit that the broadcasting monolith has feet of clay. A large amount of television comedy directs quite telling parodies at television itself. Programmes celebrating broadcasting anniversaries often show archive material that of itself helps to demystify the medium by giving present-day viewers a point of comparison. Several programmes have resurrected sequences of previously edited-out material showing disasters and mistakes occurring during the production of otherwise serious programmes. In other words the medium is to some extent self-critical, and is prepared to share its jaundiced view of itself with its audience. As a result of these developments, we in the audience are now in a position to understand and where necessary to challenge the role that television has hitherto established in society. Television is no longer *merely* a matter of myth-representation.

REFERENCES

ANNAN (1977) *Report of the Committee on the Future of Broadcasting.* London: HMSO.

BAGGALEY, J. and DUCK, S. (1976) *The Dynamics of Television.* Farnborough, Hants.: Saxon House.

BARTHES, R. (1968) *Elements of Semiology.* London: Cape.

—— (1973) *Mythologies.* London: Paladin.

—— (1977) *Image-Music-Text.* London: Fontana.

BAYNES, K. (ed.) (1971) *Scoop, Scandal and Strife.* London: Lund Humphries.

BERGER, J. (1972) *Ways of Seeing.* London: BBC/Penguin.

BERNSTEIN, B. (1973) *Class, Codes and Control* (Vol. 1). London: Paladin.

BETHELL, S. L. (1944) *Shakespeare and the Popular Dramatic Tradition.* St Albans, Herts.: Staples.

BUSCOMBE, E. (1976) '*The Sweeney* – better than nothing?', *Screen Education*, No. 20, pp. 66–9.

CULLER, J. (1976) *Saussure.* London: Fontana.

DAY, R. (1975) *Day by Day.* London: William Kimber.

DIAMOND, E. (1975) *The Tin Kazoo.* Cambridge, Mass.: M.I.T. Press.

DOMINICK, J. R. and RAUCH, G. E. (1972) 'The image of women in network TV commercials', *Journal of Broadcasting*, Vol. 16, pp. 259–65.

ECO, U. (1972) 'Towards a Semiotic Inquiry into the TV Message', *WPCS*, No. 3, pp. 103–21.

ELLIOTT, P. (1974) 'Uses and Gratifications Research: A Critique and a Sociological Alternative', in J. Blumler and E. Katz (eds) *The Uses of Mass Communications*. Beverly Hills, Calif.: Sage, pp. 249–86.

ELLIS, J. (1976) 'Semiology, Art and the Chambers Fallacy', *WPCS*, No. 9, pp. 128–31.

DE FLEUR, M. (1964) 'Occupational roles as portrayed on television', *Public Opinion Quarterly*, Vol. 28, pp. 57–74.

DE FLEUR, M. and BALL-ROKEACH, S. (1975) *Theories of Mass Communication*. New York: McKay.

GALTANG, J. and RUGE, M. (1973) 'Structuring and Selecting News', in S. Cohen and J. Young (eds) *The Manufacture of News*. London: Constable, pp. 62–72.

GERBNER, G. (1969) 'Towards "Cultural Indicators": the analysis of mass mediated public message systems', in G. Gerbner, O. Holsti, K. Krippendorf, W. Paisley and P. Stone (eds), *The Analysis of Communication Content*. New York: John Wiley, pp. 123–32.

—— (1970) 'Cultural indicators: the case of violence in television drama', *Annals of the American Association of Political and Social Science*, Vol. 338, pp. 69–81.

—— (1972) 'Communication and social environment', in *Scientific American: Communication*. San Francisco, Calif.: Freeman, pp. 112–18.

—— (1973a) 'Cultural Indicators: the third voice', in G. Gerbner, L. Gross and W. Melody (eds), *Communication Technology and Social Policy*. New York: Wiley-Interscience, pp. 555–73.

—— (1973b) 'Teacher image in mass culture: symbolic functions of the "hidden curriculum"', in Gerbner, Gross and Melody (eds), op. cit., pp. 265–86.

GLASGOW MEDIA GROUP (1976) *Bad News*. London: Routledge & Kegan Paul.

GOODY, J. and WATT, I. (1962) 'The Consequences of Literacy', in P. P. Giglioli (ed.) (1972) *Language and Social Context*. Harmondsworth: Penguin, pp. 311–57.

GREIMAS, A. J. (1966) *Sémantique Structurale*. Paris: Larousse.

GUIRAUD, P. (1975) *Semiology*. London: Routledge & Kegan Paul.

HALL, S. (1973) 'Encoding and decoding in the television discourse', Centre for Contemporary Cultural Studies, Birmingham, *Occasional Papers*, No. 7.

HARBAGE, A. (1941) *Shakespeare's Audience*. Chicago: University of Chicago Press.

HARTLEY, J. and FISKE, J. (1977) 'Myth-Representation: a cultural reading of *News at Ten*', *Communication Studies Bulletin*, Sheffield City Polytechnic, No. 4, pp, 12–33.

HAWKES, T. (1973) *Shakespeare's Talking Animals*. London: Edward Arnold.

—— (1977) *Structuralism and Semiotics*. London: Methuen.

HEAD, S. (1954) 'Content Analysis of Television Drama Programmes', *Quarterly of Film, Radio and Television*, Vol. 9, No. 2, pp. 175–94.

JAKOBSON, R. (1958) 'Closing Statement: Linguistics and Poetics', in T. A. Sebeok (ed.) (1960) *Style and Language*. Cambridge, Mass.: M.I.T .Press, pp. 350–77.

KATZ, E., GUREVITCH, M. and HASS, E. (1973) 'On the uses of mass media for important things', *American Sociological Review*, Vol. 38, pp. 164–81.

KNIGHTLEY, P. (1975) *The First Casualty*. London: André Deutsch.

KUEHN, L. L. (1976) 'The only game in town', *Pacific Sociological Review*, Vol. 19, No. 3, pp. 385–400.

LABOV, W. (1969) 'The logic of nonstandard English', in P. P. Giglioli (ed.) (1972) *op. cit.*, pp. 179–215.

LANGE, R. (1975) *The Nature of Dance*. Plymouth, Devon: MacDonald and Evans.

LARSEN, O., GREY, L. and FORBES, J. (1963) 'Goals and goal achievement methods in television content: models for anomie?', *Sociological Inquiry*, Vol. 33, pp. 180–96.

LASLETT, P. (1971) *The World We Have Lost* (2nd edn). London: Methuen.

LEACH, E. (1976) *Culture and Communication*. London: Cambridge University Press.

LEMON, L. and REIS, M. (1965) *Russian Formalist Criticism: Four Essays*. Lincoln, Nebr.: University of Nebraska Press.

LÉVI-STRAUSS, C. (1968) *Structural Anthropology*. Harmondsworth: Penguin.

––– (1973) *Tristes Tropiques*. London: Cape.

MACPHERSON, C. B. (1962) *The Political Theory of Possessive Individualism: Hobbes to Locke*. London: Oxford University Press.

MARX, K. and ENGELS, F. (1968) *Selected Works* (1 Vol.). London: Lawrence & Wishart.

MCLUHAN, H. M. (1964) *Understanding Media*. London: Routledge & Kegan Paul.

MCQUAIL, D. (ed.) (1972) *Sociology of Mass Communications*. Harmondsworth: Penguin.

MCQUAIL, D. (1975) *Communications*. London: Longmans.

MCQUAIL, D., BLUMLER, J. and BROWN, J. (1972) 'The television audience: a revised perspective', in McQuail (ed.) *op. cit.*, pp. 135–65.

MENDELSOHN, H. (1966) *Mass Entertainment*. New Haven, Conn.: College & University Press.

METZ, C. (1974) *Film Language*. London: Oxford University Press.

OPEN UNIVERSITY (1972) *Sorting them out: two essays on social differentiation*. Milton Keynes: The Open University, (E 282 Unit 10), pp. 55–140.

PARKIN, F. (1972) *Class Inequality and Political Order*. London: Paladin.

PELED, T. and KATZ, E. (1974) 'Media functions in wartime: the Israeli home front in October 1973', in J. Blumler and E. Katz (eds), *op. cit.*, pp. 49–69.

PIEPE, A., EMERSON, M. and LANNON, J. (1975) *Television and the Working Class*. Farnborough, Hants.: Saxon House.

PIERCE, C. S. (1931–58) *Collected Papers* (8 Vols). Cambridge, Mass.: Harvard University Press.

RAPOPORT, A. (1969) 'A system-theoretic view of content analysis', in G. Gerbner, O. Holsti, K. Krippendorf, W. Paisley and P. Stone (eds), *op. cit.*, pp. 17–38.

RUST, F. (1969) *Dance in Society*. London: Routledge & Kegan Paul.

SAUSSURE, F. DE (1974) *Course in General Linguistics*, (orig. pub. 1915). London: Fontana.

SEGGAR, J. and WHEELER, P. (1973) 'The world of work on television: ethnic and sex representation in TV drama', *Journal of Broadcasting*, Vol. 17, pp. 201–14.

SMITH, A. (1973) *The Shadow in the Cave*. London: George Allen & Unwin.

SMYTHE, D. (1953) 'Three years of New York television', *National Association of Educational Broadcasters*, Monitoring Study No. 6. Urbana, Ill.

STEPHENSON, W. (1967) *Play Theory of Mass Communication*. Chicago: University of Chicago Press.

THOMPSON, E. P. (1968) *The Making of the English Working Class*. Harmondsworth: Penguin.

WATT, I. (1957) *The Rise of the Novel*. Harmondsworth: Penguin.

WESTERGAARD, J. and RESLER, H. (1976) *Class in a Capitalist Society*. Harmondsworth: Penguin.

WHELDON, H. (1976) *The British Experience in Television*. London: BBC.

WILLIAMS, R. (1958) *Culture and Society*. Harmondsworth: Penguin.

—— (1974) *Television: Technology and Cultural Form*. London: Fontana.

—— (1975) *Drama in a Dramatized Society*. London: Cambridge University Press.

WRIGHT, C. R. (1964) 'Functional analysis and mass communication', in L. Dexter and D. M. White (eds) *People, Society and Mass Communications*. Glencoe, Ill.: Free Press, pp. 91–109.

—— (1975) *Mass Communications: A Sociological Approach* (2nd edn). New York: Random House.

FURTHER READING

THE range of sources from which we have drawn to construct our reading of television is to some extent indicated in the references (see previous section). Some of those works are not themselves concerned with television at all. In this section we shall guide readers to some of the many works whose central focus is the television medium. However, despite growing academic interest in this area, surprisingly little of the available material is devoted exclusively to television, and even less attempts to analyse specific programmes within a broader cultural context. The bulk of academic writing on the subject considers television in connection with the sociology and psychology of the mass media as a whole. On the other hand, there are significant areas of study, such as the sociology of the institutions and processes of broadcasting, which are complementary rather than central to our own approach. Readers can compensate for our relative neglect of such areas by consulting the relevant volumes suggested below.

I Introductory books and readers

1 *Introductory books*

BAGGALEY, J. and DUCK, S. (1976) *The Dynamics of Television*. Farnborough, Hants.: Saxon House. A fresh look at television and how we watch it; by psychologists rather than sociologists, hence it complements Wright (1975) below.

DE FLEUR, M. and BALL-ROKEACH, S. (1975) *Theories of Mass Communication*. New York: McKay. The main theories are well covered, and an attempt is made to combine them into a comprehensive 'integrated' model. To be read after Wright (1975) below.

MCQUAIL, D. (1975) *Communication*. London: Longmans. A comprehensive and stimulating book which gains much from setting mass communication in the context of communication in general.

OPEN UNIVERSITY (1977) *Mass Communication and Society*. Milton Keynes: The Open University (DE 353). A series of 15 specially written units. Well worth reading in its entirety, but some of the units are individually listed in the relevant sections below.

WRIGHT, C. R. (1975) *Mass Communications: a Sociological Approach*. New York: Random House. The most useful introductory work from an American viewpoint. Concise and readable.

2 *Readers in mass communication and television*

CATER, D. and ADLER, R. (eds) (1975) *Television as a Social Force: New Approaches to TV Criticism*. New York: Praeger. Deals with the main issues of American public concern about the uses and effects of television.

CURRAN, J., GUREVITCH, M. and WOOLLACOTT, J. (eds) (1977) *Mass Communication and Society*. London: Edward Arnold. Mainly original articles commissioned for the Open University. Recommended for its attention to 'general perspectives' and 'cultural meanings'.

DEXTER, L. A. and WHITE, D. M. (eds) (1964) *People, Society and Mass Communications*. Glencoe, Ill.: Free Press. A classic in the field, particularly on the functions of television and current affairs.

EMERY, M. C. and SMYTHE, T. C. (eds) (1974) *Readings in Mass Communication*. Dubuque, Iowa: W. C. Brown. An American reader with an emphasis on news and public affairs in the media. Wide variety of contributing styles.

MCQUAIL, D. (ed.) (1972) *Sociology of Mass Communications*. Harmondsworth: Penguin. Highly recommended, wide-ranging and comprehensive selection.

SCHRAMM, W. and ROBERTS, D. F. (eds) (1971) *The Process and Effects of Mass Communication*. Urbana, Ill.: University of Illinois Press. Massive collection, with important contributions from most of the major American authorities.

SKORNIA, H. J. and KITSON, J. (eds) (1968) *Problems and Controversies in Television and Radio*. Palo Alto, Calif.: Pacific Books. One of the minority of books which deals exclusively with broadcasting. Largely concerned with the cultural impact of broadcasting in America.

TUNSTALL, J. (ed.) (1973) *Media Sociology*. London: Constable. A standard work with wide-ranging contributions from most of the major British authorities.

II Semiotics

There have, as yet, been few semiotic studies of television. Most of the work in this area is theoretical or applied to film or literature. A good introduction to semiotics, with a comprehensive and helpful bibliography for the interested reader, is Hawkes, T. (1977) *Structuralism and Semiotics*. London: Methuen.

3 Semiotics

BARTHES, R. (1968) *Elements of Semiology*. London: Cape. A good, short, review of the main concerns and methods of the subject by an influential European scholar.

—— (1971) 'The Rhetoric of the Image', *WPCS*, No. 1, pp. 37–50. A stimulating discussion of the semiotics of photography, much of which can readily be applied to television. This paper has recently been republished with others by Barthes in *Image–Music–Text*, essays selected and translated by S. Heath (1977). London: Fontana, pp. 32–51.

—— (1973) *Mythologies*. London: Paladin. A brilliant series of essays on the cultural signification of such things as Persil and the brain of Einstein, and such activities as wrestling and literary criticism. The final chapter, 'Myth Today', is essential reading.

CULLER, J. (1976) *Saussure*. London: Fontana. An enjoyable introduction to the work of the 'European father of semiotics'.

ECO, U. (1977) *A Theory of Semiotics*. London: Macmillan A comprehensive, detailed study; essential reading for the serious student.

GEORGE, R. DE and GEORGE, F. DE (eds) (1972) *The Structuralists from Marx to Lévi-Strauss*. New York: Doubleday, Anchor Books. A collection of key writings. Contains excerpts from Lacan, Jakobson, Foucault, and other well-known figures.

GUIRAUD, P. (1975) *Semiology*. London: Routledge & Kegan Paul. A terse, thorough and tightly written book. This with Barthes (1968 and 1973) will provide a good theoretical base for the general student.

LEACH, E. (1974) *Lévi-Strauss*. London: Fontana. A clear and readable introduction to one of the most important figures in the field, by one of the leading British authorities.

LEACH, E. (1976) *Culture and Communication*. London: Cambridge University Press. A brilliant introduction to structuralist theory, from an anthropologist. Good on metaphor and metonymy, with a good bibliography.

METZ, C. (1974) *Film Language*. London: Oxford University Press. Passages of abstract theory applied to specific films: an attempt to provide a general semiotics of film. Recommended for the serious student.

MORIN, E. (1966) *New Trends in the Study of Mass Communications*. University of Birmingham: Centre for Contemporary Cultural Studies. An important early attempt to relate semiotics, structural anthropology and linguistics to the media. Advanced reading.

WOLLEN, P. (1969) *Signs and Meaning in the Cinema*. London: Secker and Warburg. An illustrated review of the main semiotic theories of film. Much of the book is directly applicable to television. A good introduction for the general student.

4 Communication theory

Communication (or information) theory provides another way of studying signs and codes that has a certain amount in common with semiotics. It is perhaps capable of only limited application, but the interested reader will find the following books worth reading.

CHERRY, C. (1957) *On Human Communication*. Cambridge, Mass.: M.I.T. Press. A good introduction to the theory, and its applications to a range of communication media.

LYONS, J. (1968) *Introduction to Theoretical Linguistics*. London: Cambridge University Press. Chapter 2 contains a brief explanation of the theory and of its use in linguistics.

PIERCE, C. R. (1962) *Symbols, Signals and Noise*. London: Hutchinson. More mathematical than Cherry (above), but a good exposition of the theory, particularly on the language of music.

5 Semiotic/textual analysis of television

The television message has only recently become a candidate for this sort of analysis, and the following studies represent a diversity both of approach and quality as a result.

BETTETINI, G. (1973) *The Language and Technique of the Film*. The Hague: Mouton. An advanced semiotic theory of film with specific reference to television techniques.

BRUNT, R. (1972) 'The Spectacular World of Whicker', *WPCS*, No. 3, pp. 6–32. A readable and telling critique of a familiar TV style, full of wry observations set into a vigorous polemic.

BUSCOMBE, E. (ed.) (1975) *Football On Television*. London: BFI Monograph. Buscombe's own contribution, 'Cultural and televisual codes in two title-sequences', pp. 16–34, is the most rewarding. It shows how 'technical' decisions are culturally determined, resulting from perceptions and choices located outside the technology.

DYER, R. (1973) *Light Entertainment*. London: BFI Monograph. How television responds to its 'situations'; provides escape; encourages fantasies.

ECO, U. (1972) 'Towards a Semiotic Enquiry into the TV Message', *WPCS*, No. 3, pp. 103–21. Useful essay, briefly setting up some theoretical criteria and methods for semiotic analysis of television.

FISKE, J. (1978) 'Television: the flow and the text', *Madog*, Vol. 1, No. 1, pp. 7–14, The Polytechnic of Wales. A cultural analysis of one evening's viewing.

HALL, S., CONNELL, I. and CURTI, L. (1976) 'The "Unity" of Current Affairs TV', *WPCS*, No. 9, pp. 51–94. The Centre for Contemporary Cultural Studies' most ambitious textual study to date, taking an edition of *Panorama* devoted to the October 1974 general election. Analyses the strategies used in political broadcasting, and provides a theoretical overview. Essential reading, but compare with the different approach to a similar subject in Pateman (below).

HALLORAN, J. D., ELLIOTT, P. and MURDOCK, G. (1970) *Demonstrations and Communication: A Case Study*. Harmondsworth: Penguin. This justly celebrated book analyses the media coverage of the anti-Vietnam war demonstration in Grosvenor Square in October 1968. The television news is fully discussed, as are viewers' reactions. Reality emerges as the self-fulfilment of media prophecies. No longer easy to obtain, but well worth reading.

HARTLEY, J. and FISKE, J. (1977) 'Myth-Representation: a Cultural Reading of *News at Ten*', *Communication Studies Bulletin*, No. 4, pp. 12–33. On the meaning and function of television messages, with detailed reference to one news bulletin.

LEECH, G. N. (1966) *English in Advertising: a linguistic study of advertising in Great Britain*. London: Longmans. A lively and well-argued book, using material from both the press and television.

LEYMORE, V. L. (1976) *Hidden Myth*. London: Heinemann. A probing structuralist analysis of contemporary advertising, particularly good on latent (anthropological) meanings.

MCLUHAN, H. M. (1967) *The Mechanical Bride*. London: Routledge & Kegan Paul. Early McLuhan conducts us through the 'folklore of industrial man' in short, witty essays. Illustrated with material from American media of the 1950s – and de-mystifying for that reason alone.

NEWCOMBE, H. (1974) *Television: The Most Popular Art*. New York: Doubleday, Anchor Books. A 'literary-critical' study of the main genres of American television. Not systematic, but recommended for the general student.

PATEMAN, T. (1974) *Television and the February General Election*. London: BFI Monograph. Brief analysis, with appendices reprinting controversies of the period. Compare with Hall *et al.* (above).

SCHRANCK, J. (1975) *Understanding Mass Media*, N.T.C., Illinois. A simple, lively, illustrated review of many of the characteristic techniques of the media.

Screen Education (1976) No. 20. The whole issue of this journal is devoted to various essays on *The Sweeney*, of varying quality. Narrative analysis, production techniques, comparisons with other series, *The Sweeney*'s ideology, etc., are discussed.

SILVERSTONE, R. (1975) 'Structural Analysis of the Television Message', paper read to the SEFT conference,

Birkbeck College, London. An analysis of *Intimate Strangers*, using techniques derived from the Russian formalist, V. I. Propp.

VAUGHAN, D. (1976) *Television Documentary Usage*. London: BFI Monograph. A practitioner shows how television and film manufacture rather than reproduce reality. Recommended.

WILLIAMS, R. (1966) *Communications* (rev. edn). London: Chatto & Windus. Chapter 3 compares press and television priorities in the presentation of news. An interesting and readable book for the beginner.

WOOLLACOTT, J. (1977) *Messages and Meanings*. Milton Keynes: The Open University (DE 353 Unit 6). Sets some interesting analysis into a methodological and theoretical framework.

6 *Content analysis*

The results of most content analysis studies of television appear in articles. These are cited in the references (previous section), and are referred to in chapter 2. The ones that best repay further study are Gerbner (1970) and (1973a), Head (1954), and Larsen *et al.* (1963). Wright (1975) gives a useful summary of the main research projects in his chapter 5 (pp. 112–38), combining a study of television with content analyses of popular writing and radio. The reader who is interested in content analysis for its own sake might consult these additional books.

BERELSON, B. (1952) *Content Analysis in Communications Research*. New York: Hafner Press. A thorough methodological approach for the serious student, by the man often regarded as the 'father' of content analysis.

BUDD, R., THORP, R. and DONOHEW, L. (1967) *Content Analysis of Communications*. London: Macmillan. Detailed, methodological and with a full bibliography.

GERBNER, G., HOLSTI, O., KRIPPENDORF, K., PAISLEY, W. and STONE, P. (eds) (1969) *The Analysis of Communi-*

cation Content. New York: John Wiley. A wide-ranging collection of authoritative papers aimed at establishing the academic respectability and potential of the method.

HOLSTI, O, (1969) *Content Analysis for the Social Sciences and Humanities*. Reading, Mass: Addison-Wesley. The most useful book for the general student who wishes to study the technique and applications of the method. It contains helpful references to a number of earlier studies.

III Audiences

7 *Viewing behaviour*

GOODHARDT, G. J., EHRENBERG, A. and COLLINS, M. (1975) *The Television Audience: Patterns of Viewing*. Farnborough, Hants.: Saxon House. A detailed survey of the amount people watch, their habits of viewing and their programme preferences. Explodes some myths. Recommended.

PIEPE, A., EMERSON, M. and LANNON, J. (1975) *Television and the Working Class*. Farnborough, Hants.: Saxon House. An interesting book on the response to television among manual workers in Portsmouth and Southampton, and on the relationship between social class and the media. Summarizes theories and provides helpful bibliographies.

ROTHMAN, L. J. and RAUTA, I. (1969) 'Towards a Typology of the Media Audience', *Journal of Market Research Society*, Vol. 11, pp. 45–69. A good example of commercially oriented research.

BBC (1975) *Audience Research Findings*. London. An annual review, showing the methods and findings of research upon which, presumably, programming decisions are made.

8 *The uses and gratifications of television*

BLUMLER, J. and KATZ, E. (eds) (1974) *The Uses of Mass Communications*. Beverly Hills, Calif.: Sage. The standard work. A number of important empirical and theoretical studies, with valuable overview by E. Katz, J. Blumler and M. Gurevitch, and a balancing critique by Elliott.

BLUMLER, J. and KATZ, E. (eds) (1975) *The Uses and Gratifications Approach to Communications Research*. Beverly Hills, Calif.: Sage. A more advanced study, required reading for the serious student.

DEMBO, R. (1973) 'Gratifications Found in Media by British Teenage Boys', *Journalism Quarterly*, Vol. 1, Pt 3, pp. 517–26. A good example of a specific application of this approach.

GREENBERG, B. S. (1970) *The Use of the Mass Media by the Urban Poor*. New York. An American study which can usefully be read with Piepe *et al.* (1975).

9 *Specific audiences*

There is a wealth of research and argument about media portrayals of particular social groups, and about those groups' access to and uses of the media. See, for instance, on race:

HARTMANN, P. and HUSBAND, C. (1974) *Racism and the Mass Media*. London: Davis-Poynter.

HUSBAND, C. (ed.) (1975) *White Media & Black Britain*. London: Arrow.

on women:

KING, J. and STOTT, M. (eds) (1977) *Is This Your Life?* London: Virago/Quartet. One chapter on women and television by C. Koerber; representatively critical and very readable.

on children/adolescents:

BROWN, R. (ed.) (1976) *Children and Television*. London: Collier Macmillan.

HALLORAN, J. D., BROWN, R. L. and CHANEY, D. C. (1970) *Television and Delinquency*. Leicester: Leicester University Press. A detailed survey and its results: advanced.

KLINE, F. G. and CLARKE, P. (eds) (1971) *Mass Communications and Youth: Some Current Perspectives*. Beverly Hills, Calif.: Sage. An American viewpoint.

NOBLE, G. (1975) *Children in Front of the Small Screen*. London: Constable/Sage. Covers the main issues.

10 *The effects of television upon the audience*

BELSON, W. A. (1967) *The Impact of Television*. St Albans, Herts.: Crosby Lockwood. Thoroughly researched studies, which seem to show more positive 'effects' than many more recent works.

GLUCKSMANN, A. (1976) *Violence on the Screen*. London: BFI Monograph. A well-argued book, concerned with both film and television.

HALLORAN, J. D. (1970) *The Effects of Television*. St Albans, Herts.: Panther. A good survey of the research in this field, with well-balanced conclusions. Recommended for the general student. The more advanced student should consult J. D. Halloran, R. L. Brown and D. C. Chaney (above), which is an impressive study explaining the complex relationships between social problems and television. Halloran shows the futility of demanding 'easy answers'.

HALLORAN, J. D. (1977) *Mass Media Effects: A Sociological Approach*. Milton Keynes: The Open University (DE 353 Unit 7). A lucid and up-to-date account of the schools of research and the controversies of 'effects' studies.

HOWITT, D. and CUMBERBATCH, G. (1975) *Mass Media, Violence and Society*. London: Elek Science. A study by psychologists, mainly devoted to television.

KLAPPER, J. T. (1960) *The Effects of Mass Communication*. Glencoe, Ill.: Free Press. The classic in this field, and still highly regarded.

The Surgeon-General's Scientific Advisory Committee on Television and Social Behavior (1972) *Volumes I–VI*. Washington, DC: US Government Printing Office. A massive collection of research reports, many contradictory, commissioned by the US government in response to mounting public concern. Summarized by L. Bogart (1972–3) 'Warning: The Surgeon-General Has Determined that TV Violence is Moderately Dangerous to Your Child's Mental Health', *Public Opinion Quarterly*, Vol. 26, pp. 491–521.

IV Television and culture

11 *The popular culture debate*

Television is the great modern anti-hero for many writers concerned about the state of health of western cultural values. The earlier expression of fairly generalized outrage has in more recent studies been modified. Television now attracts more finely focused cultural criticism, and in some quarters even approval. The following books will conduct the reader through much of the debate.

BIGSBY, C. W. (ed.) (1976) *Approaches to Popular Culture*. London: Edward Arnold. A product of more recent approaches to the debate, including that of structuralism. Bigsby supplies an overview in his introduction.

HALL, S. and WHANNEL, P. (1964) *The Popular Arts*. London: Hutchinson. One of the earliest books to take British popular culture seriously.

HARTLEY, J. and HAWKES, T. (1977) *Popular Culture and High Culture*. Milton Keynes: The Open University (DE 353 Unit 4). Places the popular versus high culture debate in a theoretical and historical perspective. Concludes with a chapter on the role of television in shaping cultural values.

MENDELSOHN, H. (1966) *Mass Entertainment*. New Haven, Conn.: College and University Press. Chapter 1 is devoted to a critical analysis of the standard attacks on mass culture. Readable and judicious. American orientation.

ROSENBERG, B. and WHITE, D. M. (eds) (1957) *Mass*

Culture: the Popular Arts in America. Glencoe, Ill.: Free Press. One of the classics; opening the debate and setting the tone (if not the standard for analytical rigour) for subsequent studies. Still highly readable, especially the irreverent contribution from L. Fiedler.

ROSENBERG, B. and WHITE, D. M. (eds) (1972) *Mass Culture Revisited.* New York: Van Nostrand Reinhold. Many of the contributors to the above compilation return to the battleground and dig up some old corpses.

THOMSON, D. (ed.) (1964) *Discrimination and Popular Culture.* Harmondsworth: Penguin. An easily available British introduction to the debate. Revised and extended edition published in 1973.

Working Papers in Cultural Studies (WPCS), a journal now produced annually by the Centre for Contemporary Cultural Studies, University of Birmingham. A sophisticated and rigorous theoretical approach is adopted towards all forms of culture. Required reading for the serious student, who should also consult the wide-ranging series of *Stencilled Occasional Papers* produced at the Centre (lists are published in *WPCS*).

12 Other cultural approaches

Many works relevant to this section will be found in the general readers, and of course there is a sense in which all television studies involve an attitude on the part of the author towards the culture which produces the message. The following books provide a sample of some of the diverse ways in which television has been seen to relate to the culture at large.

BERGER, J. (1972) *Ways of Seeing.* London: BBC/Penguin. A book derived from a series first presented on television, employing visual as well as verbal techniques. Chapter 7, on publicity, poses some challenging questions about the nature of mass-produced images in capitalist society.

COMBS, J. and MANSFIELD, M. (eds) (1976) *Drama in Life:*

the Uses of Communication in Society. New York: Hastings House. A wide and stimulating selection of articles which centre on the drama of social interaction at all levels, from the personal to mass ritual and the mass media. Recommended for the breadth of its view of what it is that our culture comprises.

GERBNER, G., GROSS, L. and MELODY, W. (eds) (1973) *Communications Technology and Social Policy: Understanding the Cultural Revolution*. New York: John Wiley. A large collection of articles on the implications of the mass media for our culture now and in the future; including the potential impact of audience-access cable television.

GOODY, J. (1977) *The Domestication of the Savage Mind*. Cambridge: Cambridge University Press. Goody continues his anthropological analysis of human culture by reference to the technology of communication, especially literacy. (See J. Goody and I. Watt, above.)

HALL, S. (1973-5) *Stencilled Occasional Papers*. University of Birmingham: Centre for Contemporary Cultural Studies. Several papers by one of Britain's leading writers in this area are devoted to television and the media: Nos 4, 5, 7, 11 and 34. Particularly recommended are: No. 5, 'The Structured Communication of Events'; No. 7, 'Encoding and Decoding in the TV Discourse'; No. 34, 'TV as a Medium and its Relation to Culture'.

MCLUHAN, H. M. (1964) *Understanding Media*. London: Routledge & Kegan Paul. McLuhan's books, which include *The Gutenberg Galaxy* (1962) and *The Mechanical Bride* (1967), (both Routledge), constitute a mine of stimulating and provocative theses about the nature of industrial culture and the formative role played by various media in shaping the social construction of reality. McLuhan suffers more than most from the bad press of fashion, but is essential reading for any student of television and culture.

STEPHENSON, W. (1967) *Play Theory of Mass Communication*. Chicago: University of Chicago Press. An unusual study, with some interesting methods and intriguing insights.

WILLIAMS, R. (1974) *Television: Technology and Cultural Form*. London: Fontana. Highly recommended book from one of the pioneers in the field. Gives a valuable historical perspective to the role of television in culture.

—— (1977) *Marxism and Literature*. Oxford: Oxford University Press. Cultural Theory comes of age. The full discussion of marxist cultural concepts, especially the Gramscian term 'hegemony', is accessible and applicable beyond purely literary studies.

13 News and current affairs

Television's potential for influence is widely held to be greatest in this area, where the medium's relationship with everyday decision-making in society is at its most direct. Hence it receives a lot of attention. The following studies will provide the reader with a range of perspectives. In addition, several of the general readers include sections specifically on this topic.

BATSCHA, R. M. (1975) *Foreign Affairs News and the Broadcast Journalist*. New York: Praeger. (The 'foreign' of course means non-American.)

COHEN, S. and YOUNG, J. (eds) (1973) *The Manufacture of News*. London: Constable. The standard work, with very high quality contributions.

COLLINS, R. (1976) *Television News*. London: BFI Monograph. Another of the British Film Institute's indispensable series of short studies.

DEXTER, L. A. and WHITE, D. M. (eds) (1964) *People, Society and Mass Communications*. Glencoe, Ill.: Free Press of Glencoe. News and current affairs studies are strongly represented in this collection, which contains D. M. White's exposition of the 'gatekeeper' theory of news selection.

DIAMOND, E, (1977) *The Tin Kazoo*, Cambridge, Mass.:

M.I.T. Press. A noted American practitioner writes a readable and well argued book.

GLASGOW MEDIA GROUP (1976) *Bad News*. London: Routledge & Kegan Paul. A very critical conclusion is reached about the 'neutrality' of the news in this study, the result of long-term surveys. Deals largely with media coverage of industrial disputes, including that of the Glasgow dustmen.

MITCHELL, A. (1973) 'The Decline of Current Affairs Television', *Political Quarterly*, (Summer) pp. 127–36. A practitioner takes a critical look at his trade.

ROSHCO, B. (1975) *Newsmaking*, Chicago: University of Chicago Press.

14 *Politics*

BLUMLER, J. G. and MCQUAIL, D. (1968) *Television in Politics: Its Uses and Influence*. London: Faber. A standard work, required reading.

BLUMLER, J. G. (1977) *The Political Effects of Mass Communication*. Milton Keynes: The Open University (DE 353 Unit 8). A lively summary of recent political effects research, critical of much of it, and setting out a vigorous re-assertion of the author's stance. Recommended reading.

SEYMOUR-URE, C. (1974) *The Political Impact of the Mass Media*. London: Constable.

A very different perspective on the political impact of the media can be had from BEHARRELL, P. and PHILO, G. (eds) (1977) *Trade Unions and the Media*. London: Macmillan.

15 *Media imperialism*

There is a growing realization among observers that one of the major export commodities produced in the west, particularly America, is the television message. The works cited below give a good overview of this area of work. Bigsby studies American influences on European culture; Schiller and Boyd-Barrett are more concerned with the third world; Tunstall, whose approach is the most comprehensive, surveys both the values of the media themselves and their world impact.

BIGSBY, C. W. (1975) *Superculture: American Popular Culture and Europe*. London: Paul Elek.

BOYD-BARRETT, O. (1977) *Mass Communications in Cross Cultural Contexts: the Case of the Third World*. Milton Keynes: The Open University (DE 353 Unit 5).

SCHILLER, H. (1970) *Mass Communications and American Empire*. Fairfield, NJ: Kelly.

TUNSTALL, J. (1977) *The Media are American*. London: Constable.

16 Institutions and processes

How the organizations that produce the messages are constituted, and their effect on the messages. This area has attracted two types of study, the sociological and the anecdotal (based on practitioners' experiences). Chaney, Elliott and Smith represent the former, while Bakewell and Garnham represent the latter. Burns demonstrates, in a major study, that the two approaches are not incompatible, using tape-recorded interviews collected in the early 1960s and 1970s as data in a sociological study of the ideologies of a unique organization.

BAKEWELL, J. and GARNHAM, N. (1970) *The New Priesthood*. Harmondsworth: Penguin.

BURNS, T. (1977) *The BBC: Public Institution and Private World*. London: Macmillan.

CHANEY, D. (1972) *The Processes of Mass Communication*. London: Macmillan.

ELLIOTT, P. R. (1972) *The Making of a Television Series*. London: Constable.

SMITH, A. (1973) *The Shadow in the Cave*. London: George Allen and Unwin.

INDEX